Weather

D1540542

TEACHER'S GUIDE

SCIENCE AND TECHNOLOGY FOR CHILDREN

NATIONAL SCIENCE RESOURCES CENTER
Smithsonian Institution • National Academy of Sciences
Arts and Industries Building, Room 1201
Washington, DC 20560

NSRC

The National Science Resources Center is operated by the Smithsonian Institution and the National Academy of Sciences to improve the teaching of science in the nation's schools. The NSRC collects and disseminates information about exemplary teaching resources, develops and disseminates curriculum materials, and sponsors outreach activities, specifically in the areas of leadership development and technical assistance, to help school districts develop and sustain hands-on science programs. The NSRC is located in the Arts and Industries Building of the Smithsonian Institution and in the Capital Gallery Building in Washington, D.C.

CB787189607

Foreword

Since 1988, the National Science Resources Center (NSRC) has been developing Science and Technology for Children (STC), an innovative hands-on science program for children in grades one through six. The 24 units of the STC program, four for each grade level, are designed to provide all students with stimulating experiences in the life, earth, and physical sciences and technology while simultaneously developing their critical thinking and problem-solving skills.

Sequence of STC Units

Grade	Life, Earth, and Physical Sciences			
1	Organisms	Weather	Solids and Liquids	Comparing and Measuring
2	The Life Cycle of Butterflies	Soils	Changes	Balancing and Weighing
3	Plant Growth and Development	Rocks and Minerals	Chemical Tests	Sound
4	Animal Studies	Land and Water	Food Chemistry	Electric Circuits
5	Microworlds	Ecosystems	Motion and Design	Floating and Sinking
6	Experiments with Plants	Measuring Time	The Technology of Paper	Magnets and Motors

The STC units provide children with the opportunity to learn age-appropriate concepts and skills and to acquire scientific attitudes and habits of mind. In the primary grades, children begin their study of science by observing, measuring, and identifying properties. Then they move on through a progression of experiences that culminate in grade six with the design of controlled experiments.

Sequence of Development of Scientific Reasoning Skills

Scientific Reasoning Skills	Grades					
	1	2	3	4	5	6
Observing, Measuring, and Identifying Properties	◆	◆	◆	◆	◆	◆
Seeking Evidence Recognizing Patterns and Cycles		◆	◆	◆	◆	◆
Identifying Cause and Effect Extending the Senses				◆	◆	◆
Designing and Conducting Controlled Experiments						◆

The "Focus–Explore–Reflect–Apply" learning cycle incorporated into the STC units is based on research findings about children's learning. These findings indicate that knowledge is actively constructed by each learner and that children learn science best in a hands-on experimental environment where they can make their own discoveries. The steps of the learning cycle are as follows:

- Focus: Explore and clarify the ideas that children already have about the topic.

- Explore: Enable children to engage in hands-on explorations of the objects, organisms, and science phenomena to be investigated.

- Reflect: Encourage children to discuss their observations and to reconcile their ideas.

- Apply: Help children discuss and apply their new ideas in new situations.

The learning cycle in STC units gives students opportunities to develop increased understanding of important scientific concepts and to develop better attitudes toward science.

The STC units provide teachers with a variety of strategies with which to assess student learning. The STC units also offer teachers opportunities to link the teaching of science with the development of skills in mathematics, language arts, and social studies. In addition, the STC units encourage the use of cooperative learning to help students develop the valuable skill of working together.

In the extensive research and development process used with all STC units, scientists and educators, including experienced elementary school teachers, act as consultants to teacher-developers, who research, trial teach, and write the units. The process begins with the developer researching the unit's content and pedagogy. Then, before writing the unit, the developer trial teaches lessons in public school classrooms in the metropolitan Washington, D.C., area. Once a unit is written, the NSRC evaluates its effectiveness with children by nationally field-testing it in ethnically diverse urban, rural, and suburban public schools. At the field-testing stage, the assessment sections in each unit are also evaluated by the Program Evaluation and Research Group of Lesley College, located in Cambridge, Mass. The final editions of the units reflect the incorporation of teacher and student field-test feedback and of comments on accuracy and soundness from the leading scientists and science educators who serve on the STC Advisory Panel.

Major support for the STC project has been provided by the National Science Foundation, the John D. and Catherine T. MacArthur Foundation, the U.S. Department of Defense, the Dow Chemical Company Foundation, and the U.S. Department of Education. Other contributors include E. I. du Pont de Nemours & Company, the Amoco Foundation, Inc., and the Hewlett-Packard Company.

Acknowledgments

The field-test edition of *Weather* was researched and developed by Debby Deal, who also did initial work on the revision of the unit. Marilyn Fenichel edited the field-test edition. The final edition of *Weather* was written by Katherine Stiles. It was edited by Dorothy Sawicki and illustrated by Max-Karl Winkler. Other NSRC staff who contributed to the development and production of the unit include Joyce Lowry Weiskopf, STC project director (1992–95); Dean Trackman, publications director; Kathleen Johnston, publications director (1989–94); Wendy Binder, research associate; Heidi M. Kupke, publications technology specialist; and Catherine Corder, publications technology specialist (1992–93). The unit was evaluated by Sabra Price, senior research associate, Program Evaluation and Research Group, Lesley College. *Weather* was trial taught in Clifton Elementary School in Clifton, VA.

The technical and educational review of *Weather* was conducted by:

Peter P. Afflerbach, Associate Professor, National Reading Research Center, University of Maryland, College Park, MD

Jessica Fuller, Teacher, Olney Elementary School, Olney, MD

Barbara G. Levine, Teacher, Early Childhood Center, Rockville, MD

Richard McQueen, Teacher/Learning Manager, Alpha High School, Gresham, OR

Alan Mehler, Professor, Department of Biochemistry and Molecular Science, College of Medicine, Howard University, Washington, DC

H. Michael Mogil, Meteorological Educator, Rockville, MD

Philip Morrison, Professor of Physics, Emeritus, Massachusetts Institute of Technology, Cambridge, MA

Phylis Morrison, Educational Consultant, Cambridge, MA

Scott Stowell, Science Curriculum Coordinator, Spokane Public School District, Spokane, WA

Lynn Strieb, Philadelphia Teachers Learning Cooperative, Philadelphia, PA

The unit was nationally field-tested in the following school sites with the cooperation of the individuals listed:

Cambridge Public Schools, Cambridge, MA
Coordinator: Melanie Barron, Coordinator of Science
Kate Crowley, Teacher, Morse School
Noreen O'Connell, Teacher, Morse School
Katherine Synnott, Teacher, Haggerty School

Idaho School District 25, Pocatello, ID
Coordinator: Marlys McCurdy, Elementary Science Adviser
Judy Flandro, Teacher, Jefferson Elementary School
Afton Latimer, Teacher, Gate City Elementary School
Judy Sorenson, Teacher, Chubbuck Elementary School

Las Cruces Public School District 2, Las Cruces, NM
Coordinator: Christopher Cook, Assistant Principal
Diane Hall, Teacher, Fairacres Elementary School
Angie Morgan, Teacher, Mesilla Elementary School
Linda Sanchez, Teacher, Mesilla Elementary School

Mercer County Schools, Princeton, WV
Coordinator: Ann Krout, Elementary Supervisor
Dona Jones, Teacher, Knob Elementary School
Marilyn Kenny, Teacher, Mercer Elementary School
Rita Lovern, Teacher, Thorn Elementary School

San Francisco Unified School District, San Francisco, CA
Coordinator: Jan Tuomi, Coordinator of City Science
May Lee, Teacher, Alamo Elementary School
Greg Martin, Teacher, Marshall Elementary School
Gilbert Valdez, Teacher, Longfellow Elementary School

U.S. Department of Defense Dependents Schools
Coordinator: Richard M. Schlenker, Science Coordinator for the Pacific
Margaret Joan Byrne, Teacher, Bob Hope Primary School, Okinawa, Japan
Cheryl Dawson, Teacher, Kadena Elementary School, Okinawa, Japan
Sally Yoshida, Teacher, Seoul American Elementary School, Seoul, Korea

The NSRC also would like to thank the following individuals for their contributions to the unit:

L. J. Benton, Consultant to Fairfax County Public Schools, Fairfax, VA

Connie Blanchard, Teacher, Clifton Elementary School, Clifton, VA

Michelle Case, Teacher, Clifton Elementary School, Clifton, VA

Joe Griffith, Director, Hands-on Science Center, Science in American Life, National Museum of American History, Smithsonian Institution, Washington, DC

Melodee Hall, Meteorologist, National Weather Service, Sterling, VA

David Hartney, Manager of Operations, Caltech Pre-College Science Initiative, Pasadena, CA

Janet Johnson, Principal, Clifton Elementary School, Clifton, VA

Eric F. Long, Staff Photographer, Office of Printing and Photographic Services, Smithsonian Institution, Washington, DC

Mary Ellen McCaffrey, Photographic Production Control, Office of Printing and Photographic Services, Smithsonian Institution, Washington, DC

Patricia McGlashan, Educational Consultant, Stonycreek, CT

Barbara J. McNaught, Warning Coordination Meteorologist, National Weather Service, Sterling, VA

Dane Penland, Chief, Special Assignments/Photography Branch, Office of Printing and Photographic Services, Smithsonian Institution, Washington, DC

Debbie Reeder, Teacher, Clifton Elementary School, Clifton, VA

The librarians and staff of the Central Reference Service, Smithsonian Institution Libraries, Washington, DC

STC Advisory Panel

Peter P. Afflerbach, Associate Professor, National Reading Research Center, University of Maryland, College Park, MD

David Babcock, Director, Board of Cooperative Educational Services, Second Supervisory District, Monroe Orleans Counties, Spencerport, NY

Judi Backman, Math/Science Coordinator, Highline Public Schools, Seattle, WA

Albert V. Baez, President, Vivamos Mejor/USA, Greenbrae, CA

Andrew R. Barron, Associate Professor of Chemistry, Harvard University, Cambridge, MA

DeAnna Banks Beane, Project Director, YouthALIVE, Association of Science-Technology Centers, Washington, DC

Audrey Champagne, Professor of Chemistry and Education, and Chair, Educational Theory and Practice, School of Education, State University of New York at Albany, Albany, NY

Sally Crissman, Faculty Member, Lower School, Shady Hill School, Cambridge, MA

Gregory Crosby, National Program Leader, U.S. Department of Agriculture Extension Service/4-H, Washington, DC

JoAnn E. DeMaria, Teacher, Hutchison Elementary School, Herndon, VA

Hubert M. Dyasi, Director, The Workshop Center, City College School of Education (City University of New York), New York, NY

Timothy H. Goldsmith, Professor of Biology, Yale University, New Haven, CT

Patricia Jacobberger Jellison, Geologist, National Air and Space Museum, Smithsonian Institution, Washington, DC

Patricia Lauber, Author, Weston, CT

John Layman, Professor of Education and Physics, University of Maryland, College Park, MD

Sally Love, Museum Specialist, National Museum of Natural History, Smithsonian Institution, Washington, DC

Phyllis R. Marcuccio, Assistant Executive Director of Publications, National Science Teachers Association, Arlington, VA

Lynn Margulis, Professor of Biology, Department of Botany, University of Massachusetts, Amherst, MA

Margo A. Mastropieri, Co-Director, Mainstreaming Handicapped Students in Science Project, Purdue University, West Lafayette, IN

Richard McQueen, Teacher/Learning Manager, Alpha High School, Gresham, OR

Alan Mehler, Professor, Department of Biochemistry and Molecular Science, College of Medicine, Howard University, Washington, DC

Philip Morrison, Professor of Physics, Emeritus, Massachusetts Institute of Technology, Cambridge, MA

Phylis Morrison, Educational Consultant, Cambridge, MA

Fran Nankin, Editor, *SuperScience Red*, Scholastic, New York, NY

Harold Pratt, Senior Program Officer, Development of National Science Education Standards Project, National Academy of Sciences, Washington, DC

Wayne E. Ransom, Program Director, Informal Science Education Program, National Science Foundation, Washington, DC

David Reuther, Editor-in-Chief and Senior Vice President, William Morrow Books, New York, NY

Robert Ridky, Associate Professor of Geology, University of Maryland, College Park, MD

F. James Rutherford, Chief Education Officer and Director, Project 2061, American Association for the Advancement of Science, Washington, DC

David Savage, Assistant Principal, Rolling Terrace Elementary School, Montgomery County Public Schools, Rockville, MD

Thomas E. Scruggs, Co-Director, Mainstreaming Handicapped Students in Science Project, Purdue University, West Lafayette, IN

Larry Small, Science/Health Coordinator, Schaumburg School District 54, Schaumburg, IL

Michelle Smith, Publications Director, Office of Elementary and Secondary Education, Smithsonian Institution, Washington, DC

Susan Sprague, Director of Science and Social Studies, Mesa Public Schools, Mesa, AZ

Arthur Sussman, Director, Far West Regional Consortium for Science and Mathematics, Far West Laboratory, San Francisco, CA

Emma Walton, Program Director, Presidential Awards, National Science Foundation, Washington, DC, and Past President, National Science Supervisors Association

Paul H. Williams, Director, Center for Biology Education, and Professor, Department of Plant Pathology, University of Wisconsin, Madison, WI

National Science Resources Center

Douglas Lapp, Executive Director
Sally Goetz Shuler, Deputy Director for Development,
  External Relations, and Outreach
R. Gail Thomas, Administrative Officer
Gail Greenberg, Executive Administrative Assistant
Richard M. Witter, Development Consultant

Publications

Dean Trackman, Director
Marilyn Fenichel, Managing Editor, STC Discovery Deck
Linda Harteker, Writer/Editor
Lynn Miller, Writer/Editor
Dorothy Sawicki, Writer/Editor
Max-Karl Winkler, Illustrator
Heidi M. Kupke, Publications Technology Specialist
Matthew Smith, Editorial Assistant
Laura Akgulian, Writer/Editor Consultant
Cynthia Allen, Writer/Editor Consultant
Judith Grumstrup-Scott, Writer/Editor Consultant
Lois Sloan, Illustrator Consultant

Science and Technology for Children Project

Patricia K. Freitag, Project Director
Judith White, Program Officer, STC Discovery Deck
Wendy Binder, Research Associate
Christopher Lyon, Research Associate
Carol O'Donnell, Research Associate
Lisa Bevell, Program Assistant
Amanda Revere, Program Aide

Outreach

Linda J. Bentley, Outreach Coordinator
Leslie J. Benton, Program Officer, Technical Assistance
Julie Clyman Lee, Program Associate

Information Dissemination

Evelyn M. Ernst, Director
Rita C. Warpeha, Resource/Database Specialist
Barbara K. Johnson, Research Associate
Sarah Lanning, Program Assistant

The above individuals were members of the NSRC staff in 1996.

Contents

Goals for *Weather*

In this unit, students' observations and activities expand their awareness of weather, its features, and its effects on their daily lives. Their experiences introduce them to the following concepts, skills, and attitudes.

Concepts

■ Weather changes from day to day and week to week.

■ Features of weather include cloud cover, precipitation, wind, and temperature.

■ Tools used to measure different features of weather include wind scales, thermometers, and rain gauges.

■ Meteorologists are scientists who study, observe, and record information about the weather and who use that information to forecast the weather.

■ Weather affects the decisions people make about the clothing they will wear and about their outside activities.

Skills

■ Observing the weather by using the senses.

■ Discussing and recording information about weather features.

■ Using simple tools to estimate wind speed and measure temperature and rainfall.

■ Observing differences in types of clouds.

■ Conducting experiments and drawing conclusions about appropriate clothing for different types of weather.

■ Organizing weather data on graphs and long-term data collection charts.

■ Interpreting and summarizing long-term weather data.

Attitudes

■ Increasing awareness of weather.

■ Appreciating how weather affects daily life.

■ Recognizing that measurements and long-term records are useful and help us learn more about weather.

Unit Overview and Materials List

Childhood is a time for wondering. Young children are typically curious and ask endless questions about their world and how it works. Their curiosity about weather may lead them to ask specific questions, but more often it may show itself in other ways. Think, for example, of a young child playing in the snow. Here, questions are probably not spoken but instead take the form of playful investigation as the child jumps in a snowdrift, watches a powdery snowball fall to pieces and a slushy one hold its shape, or blows on a snowflake and watches it melt. In whatever form the curiosity is expressed, the child is clearly seeking information.

The *Weather* unit was designed to draw upon and expand this natural curiosity and enthusiasm for finding out about weather. In doing so, it also provides a comfortable introduction to what may be students' first experience with the study of science.

Weather is a 16-lesson unit developed and successfully field-tested with first-graders. It builds on children's observational capabilities by introducing them gradually to specific weather features. As these features are presented, students discover that their own powers of observation can be extended by using tools of science—for example, the thermometer. Developing new skills such as reading the thermometer also leads them to explore some practical facets of weather as it affects their daily lives.

Lesson 1, a pre-unit assessment, acknowledges children's interest in weather by starting with a brainstorming activity that invites them to discuss what they already know about this subject. In Lesson 2, their observations become more focused as they concentrate on what their individual senses tell them about weather. In Lesson 3, students begin recording their observations on a long-term data collection device, the daily Weather Calendar. Keeping track of the weather on a daily basis lets them see how it changes from day to day and week to week.

In Lessons 4 through 14, students focus on observing, discussing, measuring, and recording data on the four weather features explored in the unit. These features are cloud cover, precipitation, wind, and temperature.

In Lesson 4, students learn how to work with a wind scale to estimate the speed of the wind. This is the first of the three simple scales they will use. The importance of scales is reinforced in Lessons 5 through 7, when students become acquainted with the Fahrenheit thermometer scale. They learn to read model and real thermometers, take daily temperature readings, and record their findings on a class Temperature Graph. They continue to practice reading thermometers in Lessons 8 and 9.

Precipitation becomes the focus of study in the next three lessons. In Lesson 10, students construct their third scale, a rain gauge, and practice measuring rainfall. In Lesson 11, they explore what happens to rain after it has fallen. An experiment in Lesson 12 provides an opportunity for students to learn about appropriate clothing for rainy weather.

In Lessons 13 and 14, students turn their attention to the fascinating diversity of cloud appearances, categorizing an assortment of cloud photographs in different ways on the basis of their observations.

By the end of the unit, students have become more experienced at measuring and recording their weather observations. They are ready to summarize the data they have collected over the course of the unit. In Lesson 15, they compare an actual weather forecast with their own data. In Lesson 16, they refer to their data to form generalizations about the weather that has occurred in their own locale since the unit began.

Following Lesson 16 is a post-unit assessment, which is matched to the pre-unit assessment in Lesson 1. In addition, final assessments provide further questions and challenges for evaluating student progress.

By the end of the unit, children will have approached weather phenomena both in ways that were already familiar to them, by using their senses, and in new ways, by using the tools of science to measure weather features and record data. Their new scientific and practical knowledge will have contributed to their understanding of weather and the way it affects their lives.

Materials List

Below is a list of the materials needed for the *Weather* unit. Please note that the metric and English equivalent measurements in this unit are approximate.

- 1   *Weather* Teacher's Guide
- *30   optional Student Notebooks (*My Weather Book*)
- 1   pkg. Post-it™ notes, 7.6 cm (3 in) square
- 3   Weather Calendars
- 1   set of 11 weather stamps (sunny, partly cloudy, cloudy, foggy, no precipitation, snow, hail, rain, no wind, some wind, strong wind)
- 1   date stamp
- 1   stamp pad
- 1   pkg. Post-it™ notes, 7.6 x 12.5 cm (3 x 5 in)
- 31   pieces of white fabric, 10 x 15 cm (4 x 6 in)
- 31   pieces of stiff tagboard, 5 x 18 cm (2 x 7 in)
- 31   Fahrenheit thermometers
- 31   red crayons
- 1   piece of poster board, 29 x 73.5 cm (11½ x 29 in)
- 1   hole punch
- 1   white shoelace, 142 cm (56 in) long
- 1   red marker
- 31   Fahrenheit thermometer backings
- 31   white shoelaces, 61 cm (24 in) long
- 3   sheets of large graph paper with 2.5-cm (1-in) squares
- 30   large plastic cups, 473 ml (16 oz)
- 10   small plastic cups, 118 ml (4 oz)
- 2   plastic pails, 3.8 liters (1 gal)
- 1   roll of transparent tape
- 15   sheets of white construction paper, 23 x 28 cm (9 x 11 in)
- 15   sheets of black construction paper, 23 x 28 cm (9 x 11 in)
- 1   roll of clear packing tape
- 8   aluminum pie plates, 20 cm (8 in) diameter

- 30   medium plastic cups, 296 ml (10 oz)
- 30   rubber bands
- 8   pieces of nylon fabric, 15 cm (6 in) square
- 8   pieces of cotton fabric, 15 cm (6 in) square
- 8   pieces of cotton-polyester fabric, 15 cm (6 in) square
- 8   pieces of wool fabric, 15 cm (6 in) square
- 30   sheets of light blue construction paper, 23 x 28 cm (9 x 11 in)
- 600   cotton balls
- 10   sets of 9 cloud photographs (3 stratus, 3 cumulus, 3 cirrus)

- **   Scissors
- **   Crayons
- **   Newsprint or poster board
- **   Colored markers
- **   Overhead transparency sheets
- **   Masking tape
- **   Glue or paste
- **   Staplers
- **   Meter stick or yardstick
- **   Paper towels or sponges
- **   Watering can or plastic milk carton
- **   Food coloring
- **   Pencils

*Note: The optional Student Notebooks are available from Carolina Biological Supply Company (1-800-334-5551).

**Note: These items are not included in the kit but are commonly available in most schools or can be brought from home.

Teaching *Weather*

The following information on unit structure, teaching strategies, materials, and assessment will help you give students the guidance they need to make the most of their hands-on experiences with this unit.

Unit Structure

How Lessons Are Organized in the Teacher's Guide: Each lesson in the *Weather* Teacher's Guide provides you with a brief overview, lesson objectives, key background information, a materials list, advance preparation instructions, step-by-step procedures, and helpful management tips. Many of the lessons include recommended guidelines for assessment. Lessons also frequently indicate opportunities for curriculum integration. Look for the following icons that highlight extension ideas:

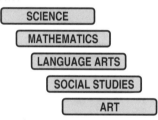

SCIENCE
MATHEMATICS
LANGUAGE ARTS
SOCIAL STUDIES
ART

Please note that all record sheets, blackline masters, student instructions, and reading selections may be copied and used in conjunction with the teaching of this unit.

Student Notebook: An optional consumable notebook, *My Weather Book,* has been published for this unit. The notebook is an individual, bound copy of all the record sheets and student instructions contained in the Teacher's Guide. (Students record weather observations, experiment results, and other individual work on the record sheets; the student instructions guide them through the steps for assembling wind flags, model thermometers, and rain gauges.)

If your class does not use student notebooks, you will need to make copies of the record sheets and student instructions from the Teacher's Guide for your students, as directed in the individual lessons.

Please note that the lessons involving temperature refer to the Fahrenheit scale. This scale is used because of students' familiarity with it; that is, they most often hear temperatures given in Fahrenheit degrees on television and radio weather reports and in other situations in their daily lives. The Fahrenheit scale is used on all record sheets that show a thermometer or ask students to read and record a temperature.

If you elect to use the Celsius scale in teaching the *Weather* unit, your class will need a Celsius version of the record sheets; you will find them in Appendix B of the Teacher's Guide. The Student Notebook, *My Weather Book,* contains record sheets for use with the Fahrenheit scale only.

Teaching Strategies

Classroom Discussion: Class discussions, effectively led by the teacher, are important vehicles for science learning. Research shows that the way questions are asked, as well as the time allowed for responses, can contribute to the quality of the discussion.

When you ask questions, think about what you want to achieve in the ensuing discussion. For example, open-ended questions, for which there is no one right answer, will encourage students to give creative and thoughtful answers. You can use other types of questions to encourage students to see specific relationships and contrasts or to help them summarize and draw conclusions. It is good practice to mix these questions. It also is good practice always to give students "wait time" to answer; this will encourage broader participation and more thoughtful answers. You will want to monitor responses, looking for additional situations that invite students to formulate hypotheses, make generalizations, and explain how they arrived at a conclusion.

Brainstorming: Brainstorming is a whole-class exercise in which students contribute their thoughts about a particular idea or problem. When used to introduce a new science topic, it can be a stimulating and productive exercise. It also is a useful and

A sample of a web

efficient way for the teacher to find out what students know and think about a topic. As students learn the rules for brainstorming, they will become more and more adept in their participation.

To begin a brainstorming session, define for students the topics about which they will share ideas. Tell students the following rules:

■ Accept all ideas without judgment.

■ Do not criticize or make unnecessary comments about the contributions of others.

■ Try to connect your ideas to the ideas of others.

Webbing: Webbing enables you to record ideas in a graphic display with the main subject at the center, or nucleus, of the web. The advantage of webbing is that it identifies relationships between related ideas and the nucleus. Webbing helps students recognize what they already know about a subject and invites them to make as many associations as they can about it. "Concept mapping" and "clustering" are other names for webbing activities. Figure T-1 illustrates a web on clouds that students create during a brainstorming session in the *Weather* unit.

Cooperative Learning Groups: One of the best ways to teach hands-on science is to arrange students in small groups. There are several advantages to this organization. It provides a small forum for students to express their ideas and get feedback. It also offers students a chance to learn from one another by sharing ideas, discoveries, and skills. With coaching, students can develop important interpersonal skills that will serve them well in all aspects of life. As students work, they will often find it productive to talk about what they are doing, resulting in a steady hum of conversation. If you or others in the school are accustomed to a quiet room, this new, busy atmosphere may require some adjustment.

Learning Centers: You can give supplemental science materials a permanent home in the classroom in a spot designated as the learning center. Students can use the center in a number of ways: as an "on your own" project center, as an observation post, as a trade-book reading nook, or simply as a place to spend unscheduled time when

assignments are done. To keep interest in the center high, change the learning center or add to it often. Here are a few suggestions of items to include:

■ Science trade books about weather in general, severe or stormy weather, seasons, and the world of meteorology (see the Bibliography for suggested titles).

■ Audiovisual materials on related subjects.

■ Items contributed by students for sharing.

Materials

Organization of Materials: To help ensure an orderly progression through the unit, you will need to establish a system for storing and distributing materials. Being prepared is the key to success. Here are a few suggestions.

■ Read through the Materials List on pg. 4. Begin to collect the items you will need that are not provided in the kit.

■ Organize your students so that they are involved in distributing and returning materials. If you have an existing network of cooperative groups, delegate the responsibility to one member of each group.

- Organize a distribution center and instruct your students to pick up and return supplies to that area. A cafeteria-style approach works especially well when there are large numbers of items to distribute.

- Look at each lesson ahead of time. Some have specific suggestions for handling materials needed that day.

- Plan to be flexible. The weather will not necessarily accommodate teaching the lessons in this unit in sequence. If necessary, the lessons listed below can be postponed and taught later in the unit when the weather is suitable.

    Lesson 4: Estimating Wind Speed
    Lesson 9: Experimenting with Color and
        Temperature
    Lesson 10: Making a Rain Gauge
    Lesson 11: Exploring Puddles
    Lesson 13: Observing Clouds

- Become familiar with the safety tips that appear in some lessons.

- Management tips are also provided throughout the unit. Look for the following icon:

Assessment

Philosophy: In the Science and Technology for Children program, assessment is an ongoing, integral part of instruction. Because assessment emerges naturally from the activities in the lessons, students are assessed in the same manner in which they are taught. They may, for example, perform experiments, record their observations, or make oral presentations. Such performance-based assessments permit the examination of processes as well as of products, emphasizing what students know and can do.

The learning goals in STC units include a number of different science concepts, skills, and attitudes. Therefore, a number of different strategies are provided to help you assess and document your students' progress toward the goals (see Figure T-2). These strategies also will help you report to parents and appraise your own teaching. In addition, the assessments will enable your students to view their own progress, reflect on their learning, and formulate further questions for investigation and research.

Figure T-2 summarizes the goals and assessment strategies for this unit. The left-hand column lists the individual goals for the *Weather* unit and the lessons in which they are addressed. The right-hand column identifies lessons containing assessment sections to which you can turn for specific assessment strategies. These strategies are summarized as bulleted items in the right-hand column.

Assessment Strategies: The assessment strategies in STC units fall into three categories: matched pre- and post-unit assessments, embedded assessments, and final assessments.

The first lesson of each STC unit is a *pre-unit assessment* designed to give you information about what the whole class and individual students already know about the unit's topic and what they want to find out. It often includes a brainstorming session during which students share their thoughts about the topic through exploring one or two basic questions. In the *post-unit assessment* following the final lesson, the class revisits the pre-unit assessment questions, giving you two sets of comparable data that indicate students' growth in knowledge and skills.

Throughout a unit, assessments are woven into, or embedded, within lessons. These *embedded assessments* are activities that occur naturally within the context of both the individual lesson and the unit as a whole; they are often indistinguishable from instructional activities. By providing structured activities and guidelines for assessing students' progress and thinking, embedded assessments contribute to an ongoing, detailed profile of growth. In many STC units, the last lesson is an embedded assessment that challenges students to synthesize and apply concepts or skills from the unit.

Final assessments can be used to determine students' understanding after the unit has been completed. In these assessments, students may work with materials to solve problems, conduct experiments, or interpret and organize data. In grades three through six, they may also complete self-evaluations or paper-and-pencil tests. When you are selecting final assessments, consider using more than one assessment to give students with different learning styles additional opportunities to express their knowledge and skills.

continued on pg. 10

Weather: Goals and Assessment Strategies

Concepts	
Goals	**Assessment Strategies**
Weather changes from day to day and week to week. Lessons 1–16	Lessons 1, 3–5 • Pre- and post-unit assessments • Class lists and charts • Class discussions • Record sheets
Features of weather include cloud cover, precipitation, wind, and temperature. Lessons 3–7, 10, 13–16	Lessons 1, 3–5, 10, 14, and Final Assessments 1–4 • Pre- and post-unit assessments • Class lists and discussions • Teacher's observations • Weather Calendar data • Class web on clouds • Record sheets
Tools used to measure different features of weather include wind scales, thermometers, and rain gauges. Lessons 4–7, 10	Lessons 4, 5, 10 • Student products: wind flag, model thermometer, rain gauge • Record sheets • Class discussions • Teacher's observations
Meteorologists are scientists who study, observe, and record information about the weather and who use that information to forecast the weather. Lessons 2, 4, 14, 15	Final Assessments 1, 2 • Class discussions • Oral presentations • Individual drawings
Weather affects the decisions people make about the clothing they will wear and about their outside activities. Lessons 1, 4–6, 9, 11, 12, 15	Lessons 1, 4, 5, 12, and Final Assessments 1–4 • Pre- and post-unit assessments • Class lists and discussions • Student experiments • Record sheets • Teacher's observations • Oral presentations • Individual drawings

Skills	
Goals	**Assessment Strategies**
Observing the weather by using the senses. Lessons 1, 2, 3	Lesson 1 • Pre- and post-unit assessments • Class lists and charts • Class discussions • Teacher's observations
Discussing and recording information about weather features. Lessons 1–16	Lessons 1, 3–5, 10, 12, 14, and Final Assessments 1–4 • Pre- and post-unit assessments • Weather Calendar data • Temperature Graph data • Class charts, lists, and graphs • Record sheets • Class discussions • Teacher's observations

Skills (continued)

Goals	Assessment Strategies
Using simple tools to estimate wind speed and measure temperature and rainfall. 　　Lessons 4–7, 10	Lesson 4, 5, 10, and Final Assessment 4 　• Student products: wind flag, model thermometer, and rain gauge 　• Record sheets 　• Class discussions 　• Teacher's observations
Observing differences in types of clouds. 　　Lessons 13, 14	Lessons 1, 14, and Final Assessments 1–4 　• Pre- and post-unit assessments 　• Class web on clouds 　• Student products: cloud pictures and individual drawings 　• Class lists and charts 　• Class discussions 　• Oral presentations
Conducting experiments and drawing conclusions about appropriate clothing for different types of weather. 　　Lessons 9, 12	Lesson 12 and Final Assessments 1, 4 　• Teacher's observations 　• Record sheets 　• Class discussions 　• Oral presentations
Organizing weather data on graphs and long-term data collection charts. 　　Lessons 3–16	Lessons 3–5, 10 　• Weather Calendar data 　• Temperature Graph data 　• Record sheets 　• Class discussions 　• Teacher's observations
Interpreting and summarizing long-term weather data. 　　Lessons 3–5, 16	Lessons 3–5 　• Class discussions 　• Record sheets 　• Teacher's observations

Attitudes	
Goals	**Assessment Strategies**
Increasing awareness of weather. 　　Lessons 1–16	Lessons 1, 12, 14 　• Pre- and post-unit assessments 　• Class discussions 　• Teacher's observations
Appreciating how weather affects daily life. 　　Lessons 1, 5, 6, 9, 12, 15	Lessons 1, 5, 12, and Final Assessment 1 　• Pre- and post-unit assessments 　• Class lists and discussions 　• Record sheets 　• Teacher's observations 　• Oral presentations
Recognizing that measurements and long-term records are useful and help us learn more about weather. 　　Lessons 3–7, 10, 15–16	Lessons 3–5, 10, and Final Assessments 1–3 　• Class discussions 　• Record sheets 　• Teacher's observations 　• Oral presentations

continued from pg. 7

Documenting Student Performance: In STC units, assessment is based on your recorded observations, students' work products, and oral communication. All these documentation methods combine to give you a comprehensive picture of each student's growth.

Teachers' *observations and anecdotal notes* often provide the most useful information about students' understanding, especially in the early grades when some students are not yet writing their ideas fluently. Because it is important to document observations used for assessment, teachers frequently keep note cards, journals, or checklists. Many lessons include guidelines to help you focus your observations. The blackline master on pg. 11 provides a format you may want to use or adapt for recording observations. It includes this unit's goals for science concepts and skills.

Work products, which include both what students write and what they make, indicate students' progress toward the goals of the unit. Children produce a variety of written materials during a unit. Record sheets, which include written observations, drawings, graphs, tables, and charts, are an important part of all STC units. They provide evidence of each student's ability to collect, record, and process information. Students' science journals are another type of work product. In first and second grades, journal writings are suggested as extension activities in many lessons. Often a rich source of information for assessment, these journal writings reveal students' thoughts, ideas, and questions over time.

Students' written work products should be kept together in folders to document learning over the course of the unit. When students refer back to their work from previous lessons, they can reflect on their learning. In some cases, students do not write or draw well enough for their products to be used for assessment purposes, but their experiences do contribute to the development of scientific literacy.

Oral communication—what students say formally and informally in class and in individual sessions with you—is a particularly useful way to learn what students know. This unit provides your students with many opportunities to share and discuss their own ideas, observations, and opinions. Some young children may be experiencing such activities for the first time. Encourage students to participate in discussions, and stress that there are no right or wrong responses. Creating an environment in which students feel secure expressing their own ideas can stimulate rich and diverse discussions.

Individual and group presentations can give you insights about the meanings your students have assigned to procedures and concepts and about their confidence in their learning. In fact, a student's verbal description of a chart, experiment, or graph is frequently more useful for assessment than the product or results. Questions posed by other students following presentations provide yet another opportunity for you to gather information. Ongoing records of discussions and presentations should be a part of your documentation of students' learning.

Weather: Observations of Student Performance

STUDENT'S NAME:

Concepts	**Observations**
• Weather changes from day to day and week to week. • Features of weather include cloud cover, precipitation, wind, and temperature. • Tools used to measure different features of weather include wind scales, thermometers, and rain gauges. • Meteorologists are scientists who study, observe, and record information about the weather and who use that information to forecast the weather. • Weather affects the decisions people make about the clothing they will wear and about their outside activities.	

Skills

• Observing the weather by using the senses.

• Discussing and recording information about weather features.

• Using simple tools to estimate wind speed and measure temperature and rainfall.

• Observing differences in types of clouds.

• Conducting experiments and drawing conclusions about appropriate clothing for different types of weather.

• Organizing weather data on graphs and long-term data collection charts.

• Interpreting and summarizing long-term weather data.

Sharing What We Know about Weather

Overview and Objectives

This introductory lesson will provide you with a pre-unit assessment of your students' current knowledge of weather. Students' discussion of the day's weather and how they decide what to wear will give you a sense of their awareness of weather and how it affects their daily lives. Comparing this discussion with a parallel discussion at the end of the unit will help you assess the growth in their knowledge. As students describe today's weather in Lesson 1, they are introduced to the idea that they can learn more about weather through observation. This activity sets the stage for Lesson 2, when they begin to observe weather features and record information about them more formally.

- Students observe and describe today's weather.

- Students discuss how they decide what to wear to school each day.

- Students organize information about their favorite types of weather on a class graph.

Background

Weather affects all of us—even very young children—almost every day. First-graders, who are experienced at observing their surroundings informally, will already have some ideas of their own about weather. Lesson 1 is designed to give you a sense of how your students understand weather as the unit begins.

By asking students the first pre-assessment question—"What is the weather like today?"—you will focus class discussion on a specific topic, instead of opening a discussion of weather in general. In response to the question, students will begin to share their observations about today's weather. As this process of observing the daily weather develops over the course of the unit, students will acquire a clearer sense of how weather changes. The activities in Lesson 1 will also help prepare them to make more formal observations of the weather during the rest of the unit.

You may discover that students do not make clear distinctions between the signs of weather and other observations of nature, seasons, and holidays. For example, when asked what the weather is like today, they may respond, "The leaves are brown," or "It's almost winter." As they practice observing various features of the weather throughout the unit, however, you can expect their observations to reflect actual weather conditions much more regularly.

Your students' responses to the second pre-unit assessment question—"How do you decide what to wear to school each day?"—may reflect little decision making on their part. For example, some students may say that someone in their family selects their clothes for them, and others may not even think about what they wear. However, by the end of the unit, their responses to the same question may reflect an increased awareness of the clothing they might want to wear in different types of weather.

As the unit begins, some students may not have much to say in response to these pre-unit assessment questions, especially if they have had little experience in group discussions. However, by the end of the unit, they may be able to share their observations much more readily and in greater detail.

Materials

For each student
- 1 Post-it™ note, 7.6 cm (3 in) square
  Crayons

For the class
- 3 sheets of newsprint
- 1 marker

Preparation

1. At the top of one sheet of newsprint, write "Date," "Time," and "Location," with blanks for recording the date, time of day, and place the weather is observed. Also write the title on the chart—"What is the weather like today?"

2. On the second sheet of newsprint, write today's date and the question, "How do you decide what to wear to school each day?"

3. On the third sheet of newsprint, create a graph with the title, "Our Favorite Weather." Figure 1-1 illustrates this graph.

4. You may find it helpful to copy the poem "It's Hot" (see **Procedure,** Step 1) on a large sheet of newsprint so that students can see the poem as it is read aloud.

Procedure

1. Read the poem "It's Hot," by Shel Silverstein, to the class.

   It's Hot

   It's *hot!*
   I can't get cool,
   I've drunk a quart of lemonade.
   I think I'll take my shoes off
   And sit around in the shade.

   It's *hot!*
   My back is sticky,
   The sweat rolls down my chin.
   I think I'll take my clothes off
   And sit around in my skin.

   It's *hot!*
   I've tried with 'lectric fans,
   And pools and ice cream cones.
   I think I'll take my skin off
   And sit around in my bones.

   It's *still* hot!

   Reprinted, with permission, from *A Light in the Attic* (New York: HarperCollins Publishers, 1981), pg. 84. ©1981 Shel Silverstein.

Figure 1-1

Graph to show
students' favorite
weather

2. Ask students to briefly compare today's weather with the weather described in the poem. Then explain that for the next several weeks the class will be studying weather.

3. Start the brainstorming session by asking students to discuss the question "What is the weather like today?" with a partner. Then encourage each pair of students to share their observations with the rest of the class.

4. On the chart "What is the weather like today?" fill in the date and time of day observations are made and the name of your town or city. Record students' observations; if more than one student says the same thing (for example, "It's cold this morning"), record the observation only once, but put a check mark next to it for each repetition. Figure 1-2 illustrates a chart filled in with observations; some have check marks indicating that they were repeated.

5. Ask students how they decide what to wear to school each day. Encourage them to think about how they decided to wear the clothes they have on. Record their responses on the newsprint chart.

6. Save both pre-unit assessment charts for use at the end of the unit.

Figure 1-2

Student observations about today's weather

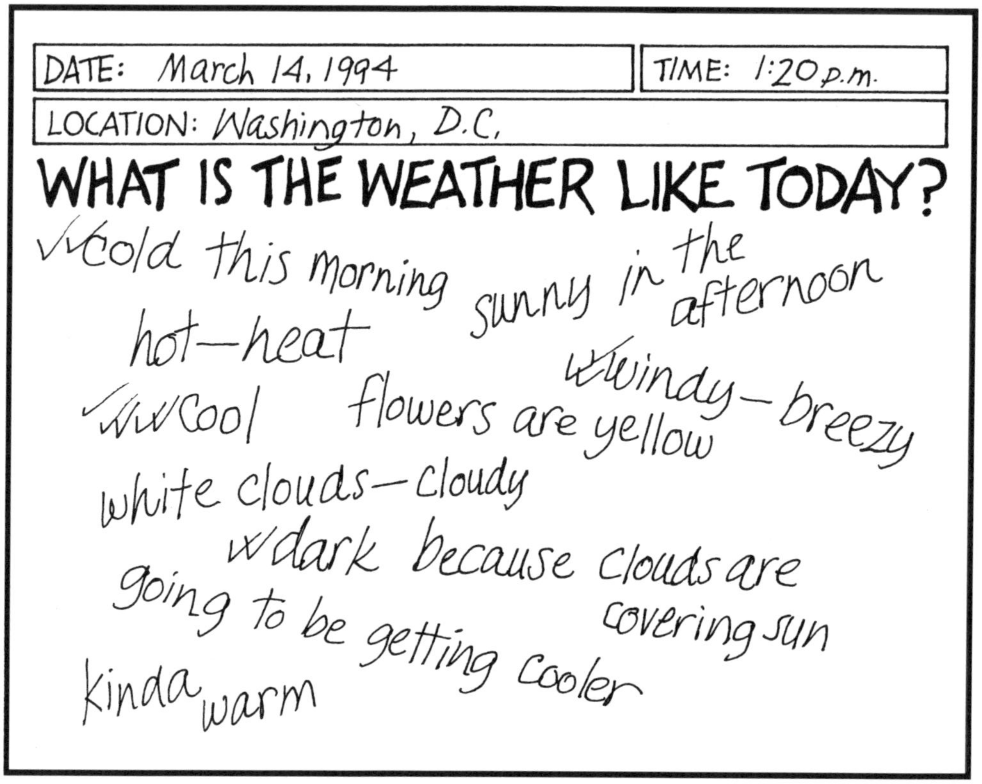

DATE: March 14, 1994   TIME: 1:20 p.m.

LOCATION: Washington, D.C.

WHAT IS THE WEATHER LIKE TODAY?

✓cold this morning   sunny in the afternoon

hot—heat   ✓✓windy—breezy

✓✓cool   flowers are yellow

white clouds—cloudy

✓dark because clouds are covering sun

going to be getting cooler

kinda warm

Final Activities

1. Show students the graph "Our Favorite Weather," and read the words "Hot," "Warm," and "Cold." Let them know that they will complete the graph to show which kinds of weather the class likes best.

2. Invite students to discuss the different kinds of clothing they wear for different kinds of weather—hot, cold, rainy, snowy.

3. Give students crayons and one Post-it™ note each. Ask them to draw a picture of themselves dressed for the kind of weather they like best.

4. Have students put their self-portraits in the appropriate columns on the graph. (They might also enjoy seeing what kind of weather you like best.)

5. When students are finished, ask them to help you count the pictures in each column. Record this number on the graph.

6. Write one or more sentences summarizing the data on the graph. For example: We have __[twenty-two]__ students in our class. __[Seven]__ like cold weather best. __[Twelve]__ like hot weather best. __[Three]__ like warm weather best. Our class likes __[hot]__ weather best.

Extensions

[MATHEMATICS]

1. Have students make a class graph showing how many prefer wet and how many prefer dry weather, or have them make a graph showing their favorite activities in their favorite weather, such as swimming in hot weather or sledding in cold weather.

[LANGUAGE ARTS]

2. Students may enjoy looking through a book such as *Weather Words*, by Gail Gibbons, which illustrates and defines some basic terms.

   Note: See the Bibliography for the full citation and an annotation for each book mentioned in this unit.

Figure 1-3

Clothes for different types of weather

Assessment

In the section entitled "Teaching *Weather*," on pgs. 5–11, you will find a detailed discussion about the assessment of students' learning. The specific goals and related assessments for this unit are summarized in Figure T-2, "*Weather*: Goals and Assessment Strategies," on pgs. 8–9.

In this lesson, the brainstorming charts entitled "What is the weather like today?" and "How do you decide what to wear to school each day?" are the first half of the matched pre- and post-unit assessments, which are important components of the assessment of your students' growth and learning. (The Post-Unit Assessment is on pgs. 157–158, following Lesson 16.)

One of the most powerful ways to assess young children's progress is by direct observation. Guidelines to help you assess your students' growth are provided in many other lessons, but you may also want to refer back to the guidelines in this first lesson from time to time.

Observational Guidelines

One goal of this unit is for students to become more aware of the weather and how it affects their lives. To help you assess the growth of your students' awareness throughout the unit, it is particularly helpful to observe the following:

- Which features of the weather your students mention during class discussions

- Whether students' observations become more specific as the unit progresses

- Whether students mention the weather spontaneously

- Whether students refer to different senses when they describe the weather

- Whether students describe ways in which the weather affects their lives

- Whether students' comments reflect their awareness that weather changes from day to day

Observing the Weather

Overview and Objectives

Now that students' attention is focused on observing the weather, Lesson 2 helps them discover how they can use their senses of sight, hearing, smell, and touch to find out more about the weather. After reading about a National Weather Service meteorologist, students relate their observations to the way scientists observe weather. These experiences prepare them for Lesson 3, when they begin to record weather data on a daily basis, just as meteorologists do.

- Students use their senses to observe the weather.

- Students discuss and record data about observable weather features.

- Students brainstorm questions they have about weather.

- Students read about and discuss how meteorologists study the weather.

Background

Weather can be defined as the "state of the atmosphere with respect to heat or cold, wetness or dryness, calm or storm, clearness or cloudiness" (*Webster's Tenth New Collegiate Dictionary*). Changes in the weather are the result of changes in the **atmosphere**, which is the blanket of air that surrounds the earth. The sun fuels these changes. It heats up the air, causing variations in temperature; these variations create movement in the air, making winds blow. The sun also draws moisture from the earth's oceans and rivers, from which clouds and precipitation develop.

In this unit students observe and record the weather variables of cloud cover, precipitation, wind, and temperature. Meteorologists at the National Weather Service use these variables and several others to make their forecasts. (Your class will learn more about meteorologists and the work they do from the reading selection "Observing the Weather with a Meteorologist," on pg. 26.)

In Lesson 2, your students may still confuse signs of weather with observations of nature, seasons, and holidays. For example, they may think of the Fourth of July as "hot weather," or may say that they hear crickets or smell flowers as they describe their observations. It is not necessary to correct such observations at this early stage. As the unit progresses, you will notice the growth in their ability to make these distinctions.

Note: You will see that Record Sheet 2-A: Weather Observations is included in the Materials list in this lesson. Your class may be using the Student Notebook, *My Weather Book,* which contains all the record sheets and student instructions for the unit. If not, you will need to make copies of these sheets, which are found at the end of the lessons in which they appear.)

Materials

For each student
    1   copy of **Record Sheet 2-A: Weather Observations**

For the class
    1   copy of the blackline master **The Four Senses**
    2   sheets of newsprint
    1   overhead transparency of Record Sheet 2-A (optional)
       Transparent tape

Preparation

1.   On one sheet of newsprint, write the title "Weather Observations." Make one copy of the blackline master **The Four Senses,** on pg. 31. Cut out the pictures and tape them to the sheet of newsprint to create a class chart like the one shown in Figure 2-1.

2.   On the other sheet of newsprint make a chart entitled "Questions We Have about Weather."

Figure 2-1

Chart ready for class use

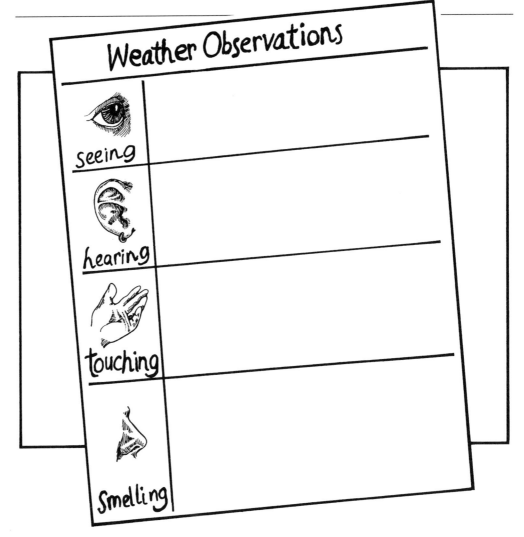

3. Make one copy for each student of **Record Sheet 2-A: Weather Observations,** on pg. 30. You may want to make an overhead transparency of this record sheet to use for recording students' observations as a class instead of having students record their observations individually.

4. Identify a location outside where you can take the students to see the sky and observe the wind moving through plants and trees. Plan to take the class outside when other students are not using the playground.

Procedure

1. Ask students to identify each of their senses and discuss the kind of information they get from each one.

> **Safety Tip**
>
> Inform students that the sense of taste is not used in science class but that the other four senses can be used to observe.

2. Use the following poem, "Who Has Seen the Wind?" by Christina Rossetti, to introduce a discussion about how we take in weather information through our senses.

Who Has Seen the Wind?

Who has seen the wind?
Neither I nor you:
But when the leaves hang trembling,
The wind is passing through.
Who has seen the wind?
Neither you nor I:
But when the leaves bow down their heads,
The wind is passing by.

Reprinted, with permission, from *Random House Book of Poetry for Children* (New York: Random House, 1983), pg. 27.

3. Now take the students outside to have them observe the weather using their senses (e.g., looking up and observing the sky; noticing whether their skin feels hot, warm, or cold; listening to the wind; or smelling the rain).

> **Safety Tip**
>
> Tell students not to look directly into the sun because it can be harmful to their eyes. Also, if you plan to have your students outside for 20 minutes or more, you might want to have them wear protective sunscreen and hats.

4. When you return to the classroom, distribute one copy of **Record Sheet 2-A: Weather Observations** to each student. Ask them to draw pictures of something they noticed about the weather or to write about what they observed while they were outside.

5. Ask students to share their observations with the class. Record these observations on the class chart, "Weather Observations." Figure 2-2 illustrates some student responses.

Figure 2-2

Student
observations
recorded on
the chart

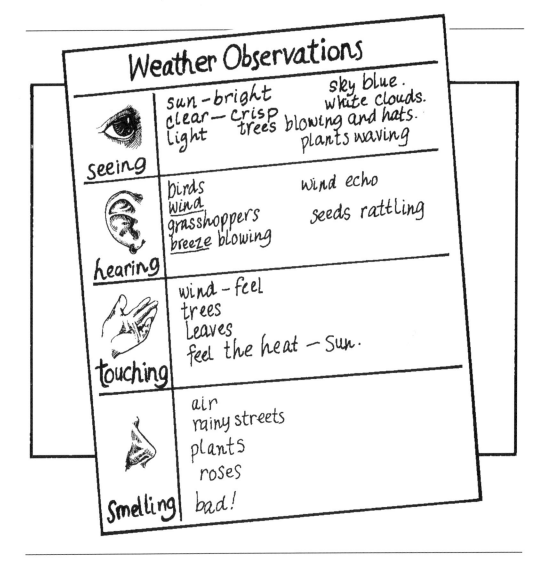

6. Help students name the various weather features that they observed, such as rain, snow, sunshine, clouds, or wind. Encourage the class to discuss their observations by asking which sense they used most frequently. Ask students whether they used more than one sense to observe the same weather feature—for example, feeling, hearing, and seeing rain.

7. Leave the class chart "Weather Observations" out where students can see it as the unit progresses. Students may want to add more observations later.

Final Activities

1. Invite students to brainstorm questions they have about the weather. Record their questions on the "Questions We Have about Weather" chart.

2. Let students know that a meteorologist is a person who can answer many questions about weather. To introduce them to the work that meteorologists do, read **"Observing the Weather with a Meteorologist,"** on pg. 26. Tell your students that Barbara McNaught is a real meteorologist whose office is at the National Weather Service in Sterling, Virginia; she was interviewed for this reading selection.

Figure 2-3

*Using senses to
observe the
weather*

3. After reading "Observing the Weather with a Meteorologist," have students discuss some of the following questions:

   ■ How does Barbara McNaught use her senses to observe the weather?

   ■ What is another way a meteorologist finds out about weather?

   ■ What senses might tell you that a thunderstorm is on the way?

4. Ask students if the story about Barbara McNaught answered any of their questions about weather. Record any additional questions they may have on the chart. Keep this chart in a place where students can add to it when they have more questions.

Extensions

SCIENCE

SCIENCE

LANG ARTS ART

LANGUAGE ARTS

SCIENCE

1. Invite a meteorologist to visit your class. Have students ask the meteorologist to discuss the questions they recorded in this lesson.

2. For a take-home activity, have students fill out **Record Sheet 2-A** on rainy, snowy, or windy days. You could also send home with students a copy of "Observing the Weather with a Meteorologist" to share with their families.

3. Read a book about stormy weather, such as *City Storms,* by Mary Jessie Parker. Then have students use watercolors to paint pictures of storms and have them dictate a sentence or two about their pictures. These illustrations can make a colorful bulletin board or class book.

4. To reinforce the idea of observing the weather, read books such as *Rain Talk,* by Mary Serfozo, or *Listen to the Rain,* by Bill Martin and John Archambault.

5. Discuss safety tips for types of severe weather, such as tornadoes or hurricanes, that might occur in your area. You can contact the National Weather Service, the American Red Cross, the Federal Emergency Management Agency, or your state or local emergency services office for more information about disaster safety.

Observing the Weather with a Meteorologist

Do you like to hear thunder?
Do you like to watch lightning from a safe place?
Barbara McNaught did when she was your age.
"I was kind of scared by thunderstorms," says Barbara,
"but I liked to watch the lightning. It reminded me of fireworks."

Now Barbara is a meteorologist. She is a weatherwoman!
Her job is to study and forecast the weather.
Barbara works at the National Weather Service.
That's one of the biggest weather watchers in the world.

Meteorologists are at work at the National Weather Service all day and all night. Even when you're asleep, they are keeping an eye on the weather. That way, if a big rainstorm or a snowstorm or a heat wave is coming your way, a weather report can tell you and your family about it ahead of time.

How does a meteorologist "keep an eye on the weather"? By looking out the window? Well, that's one way! Just as you are learning to do, Barbara uses her eyes and ears and nose and sense of touch to tell what the weather is doing.

She also uses special instruments. One of these instruments is called a thermometer. It measures the temperature to tell us how hot or cold it is.

Barbara talks to other meteorologists at the National Weather Service. They tell her about the weather patterns they have been watching.

All these different kinds of information help Barbara know what the weather is like. They also help her make weather forecasts to tell people what kind of weather is on the way—afternoon showers, or a foggy morning, or maybe even a tornado!

Are the weather forecasts that Barbara makes always right?
If she forecasts rain, will it rain for sure?
Well, not always. The weather can be very tricky.
Sometimes it can fool even meteorologists.

Barbara liked to watch storms when she was your age.
Now she is an expert in what we call "severe weather,"
weather such as hurricanes and tornadoes.
In classes called "Skywarn," she teaches people how to get ready
for storms and how to stay safe in bad weather.

She also teaches them how to spot signs of severe weather.
These people then become volunteer "spotters" for the National
Weather Service. A spotter who sees a tornado coming will call
Barbara up right away.

You can practice being a spotter by watching the weather. It's true that meteorologists use special instruments to do this, but Barbara says, "As good as those instruments are, nothing beats the human eye."

So keep your eye on the weather. Maybe one day you'll be a meteorologist, just like Barbara McNaught.

Record Sheet 2-A

Name: ----------------------------------

Date: ----------------------------------

Weather Observations

Record your observations of the weather.

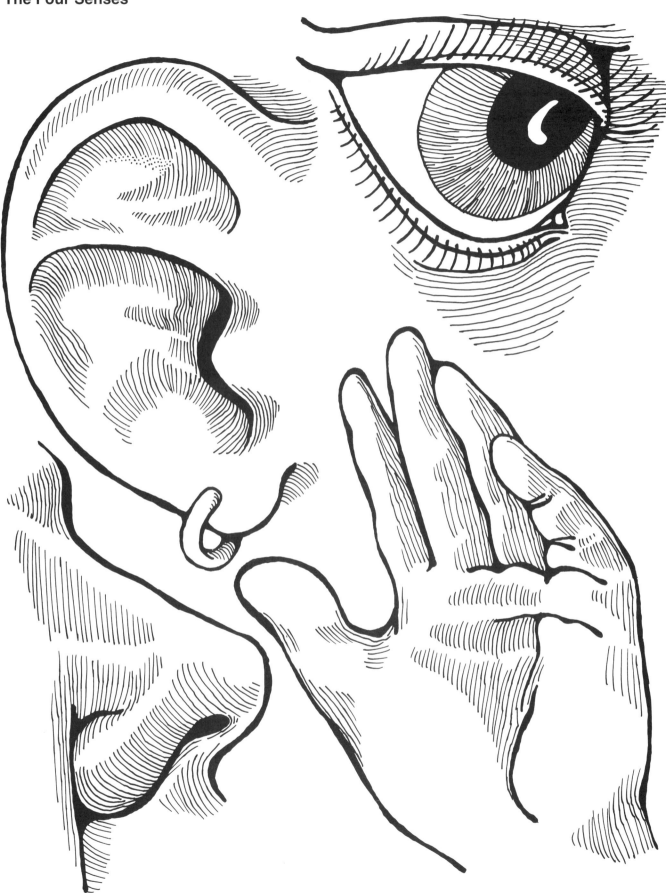

Recording the Weather

Overview and Objectives

Students began observing and describing the weather in the first two lessons. To improve their ability to observe the weather, they now focus on two basic weather features: cloud cover and precipitation. Recording observations on a daily Weather Calendar introduces students to long-term data collection. At the end of the unit, students will summarize the weather data they have collected.

■ Students observe and discuss cloud cover and precipitation.

■ Students collect data about cloud cover and precipitation.

■ Students record weather data on a calendar.

Background

In the *Weather* unit, students observe and measure four variables that meteorologists work with—cloud cover, precipitation, wind, and temperature. They have many opportunities to observe these variables and to record and interpret their weather data, first gathering information with their senses and later on using simple weather instruments.

In Lesson 3, students are introduced to the Weather Calendar, on which they will record their weather data for the rest of the unit. The Weather Calendar provides a simple and understandable way for children to participate in long-term data collection and analysis, much as scientists do.

At the end of the unit, students will use the data they collect in order to summarize their observations of the weather. At that time, for example, they may discover that during the weeks they recorded the daily weather, it was mostly cold and rainy, or that it stayed quite hot and dry, or that it varied considerably.

Materials

For the class

    3 Weather Calendars

    1 set of 11 weather stamps

    1 date stamp

    1 stamp pad

100 Post-it™ notes, 7.6 x 12.5 cm (3 x 5 in)

Preparation

1. Write the name of the current month and the year in the blank space at the top of one of the Weather Calendars. Use the other two calendars as needed for the rest of the unit.

2. Choose a place in the classroom to display the Weather Calendar. Select a spot where there is enough space for the class to gather around the calendar to discuss daily weather observations.

3. Decide on a system for having individual students take turns observing and recording the weather for the class during the rest of the unit. Various possibilities are suggested in the box below.

Recording the Weather Daily

You can integrate the Weather Calendar into your daily calendar activities. For example, you may already be reviewing days of the week and dates by using sentences such as these: "Today is __[Wednesday, October 24th]__ . Yesterday was __[Tuesday, October 23rd]__ . Tomorrow will be __[Thursday, October 25th]__ ." This would be a natural time to talk about today's, yesterday's, and tomorrow's weather.

You will need to select an effective system for assigning students to observe and record the weather on a daily basis. Here are some possibilities:

■ Appoint a team of two or more students for each week. Have one student collect the data and another record these observations for the class on the Weather Calendar.

■ Assign a different student each day to observe and use the weather stamps to record the observations of the day's weather.

■ Ask the children as a class or in small groups to describe the weather, and then select one student to record the day's weather.

■ Assign one student to observe and record the weather over weekends and holidays. You would need to make two copies of the weather stamps (Figure 3-1) to send home with the student, who would circle the stamps illustrating the weather.

So that students will be able to summarize their data at the end of the unit, try to have them observe the weather at the same time each day and perhaps put the time of day the observations were made on each day's Post-it™ note. In some areas, and especially during some seasons, the weather will change during the day. If this happens during the time your class is keeping its Weather Calendar, you might want to have the students observe and record the weather twice during the same day.

Procedure

1. Ask the question "What was the weather like two weeks ago?" Students probably will not remember exactly what it was like unless something dramatic like a major snowstorm happened. Ask students to describe today's weather. Finally, ask them to discuss how they might be able to remember today's weather two weeks from now.

2. Introduce the Weather Calendar as one way to keep track of the daily weather. Show students the weather stamps, the date stamp, and the Post-it™ notes. Starting today, they will observe the weather and record

their observations using the weather stamps on a Post-it™ note, which will then be attached to the Weather Calendar. (The system that you have selected for making these assignments can be explained to the class later; see **Final Activities,** Step 4, on pg. 36).

3. Discuss the 11 weather stamps, pictured in Figure 3-1, in more detail with the class. As you show them the stamps, let them know that they will use the wind stamps in the next lesson. The three groups of stamps are

    ■ Cloud cover (sunny, partly cloudy, cloudy, foggy)

    ■ Precipitation (no precipitation, snow, hail, rain)

    ■ Wind (no wind, some wind, strong wind)

4. Now take your class outside to observe today's weather. Ask students to pay attention to cloud cover and precipitation.

Final Activities

1. When you return to the classroom, ask students to decide which stamp best illustrates the cloud cover today. Select one student to use that stamp on a Post-it™ note.

Figure 3-1

The 11 weather stamps

CLOUD COVER

SUNNY — PARTLY CLOUDY — CLOUDY — FOGGY

PRECIPITATION

  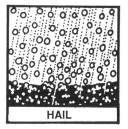 

NO PRECIPITATION — SNOW — HAIL — RAIN

WIND

NO WIND — SOME WIND — STRONG WIND

2. Ask the class to decide which stamp best illustrates today's precipitation and have one student stamp the same Post-it™ note with that stamp.

3. Finally, show the class the date stamp, and choose one student to stamp the date on the Post-it™ note. Then stick the Post-it™ note to the Weather Calendar. Figure 3-2 shows how a partially completed Weather Calendar looks as students record data.

4. End the lesson by explaining to students the system you have devised (see **"Recording the Weather Daily,"** on pg. 34) so that each student will have a turn observing and recording the weather for the class.

Figure 3-2

Recording data on the Weather Calendar

Extensions

1. Diagrams are a good way to help students summarize the weather. Figure 3-3 illustrates one way to make a lively diagram. To fill it in, have students refer to the Weather Calendar at the end of the week to see what the weather was like each day. Students would then record the sunny days inside the sun, the rainy days in the umbrella, and the cloudy days in the cloud. You could add to or modify this type of diagram as needed to match the weather in your geographic area.

Figure 3-3

Summarizing weather data on a diagram

2. Set up a learning center where students can use the weather stamps. Have students make a sample of all 11 stamps on a sheet of paper to show and discuss with their families. This helps introduce their families to the topic that your students will be studying for the next few weeks.

ART

3. Have students make large stuffed clouds, raindrops, or suns to hang around the room. They can also use the stuffed objects to create a mobile. Children can easily make these objects by cutting out two pre-drawn patterns of each weather element and gluing them together at the edges, leaving an opening for stuffing them with cotton or paper.

Assessment

Observational Guidelines

In this lesson students started recording daily observations on the Weather Calendar. To help them learn how to analyze their data, ask questions that encourage them to make comparisons and synthesize information. Throughout the rest of the unit, notice changes in your students' recording and analyzing skills.

Following are some questions that you might ask your students:

- How many days this week were sunny?
- How many days this week were cloudy?
- Were there more sunny or rainy days last week?
- What was special about the weather on [select a day of the week]?
- Which days this week had similar weather?
- On which day did you most enjoy the weather? Why?

Note: The weather will not necessarily accommodate teaching the lessons in this unit in sequence. If necessary, the following lessons can be postponed and taught later in the unit when the weather is suitable:

- Lesson 4: Estimating Wind Speed
- Lesson 9: Experimenting with Color and Temperature
- Lesson 10: Making a Rain Gauge
- Lesson 11: Exploring Puddles
- Lesson 13: Observing Clouds

Estimating Wind Speed

| **Overview and Objectives** | In Lesson 3, students observed and discussed cloud cover and precipitation. In this lesson their growing knowledge of weather develops further as they focus on a third weather feature, wind. Making a wind flag to use with a simple wind scale enables them to observe and estimate the speed of the wind. This activity also introduces students to the first of three scales they will use in this unit. By recording their wind observations on the Weather Calendar, students acquire a more complete picture of the daily weather. |

- Students describe how they know when the wind is blowing.

- Students observe and describe a flag moving in the wind.

- Students discuss and record the speed of the wind.

- Students apply a wind scale to the movement of the flag.

Background

Any sailor or kite flyer can attest to the importance of knowing about wind speed and direction. Meteorologists also need to know about these wind features in order to forecast the weather. They use weather vanes to determine the wind's direction, and to measure its speed they use an instrument called an **anemometer** (this instrument spins in the wind; the speed of the wind is determined from the rate of spin).

Meteorologists also use the **Beaufort scale,** shown in Figure 4-1, to estimate wind speed. Designed by scientists, this scale gives a numerical value to wind variations, ranging from 0 (less than 1 mile per hour) to 12 (the hurricane force of a wind 74 or more miles per hour). The scale is based on the movement of flags, trees, and chimney smoke.

Your students will observe the movement of a flag to determine the speed of the wind. Because first-graders may find the Beaufort scale too complex, they will use a simplified version—the class wind scale shown in Figure 4-2. They will collect their data by using the class wind scale and a wind flag, which is the first of several tools that will extend their senses as they observe the weather.

Materials

For each student
- 1 copy of **Student Instructions for Making a Wind Flag**
- 1 copy of **Record Sheet 4-A: Wind Data Graph**
- 1 piece of white fabric, 10 x 15 cm (4 x 6 in)
- 1 piece of stiff tagboard, 5 x 18 cm (2 x 7 in)
- Crayons

Figure 4-1

How windy is it?

THE BEAUFORT SCALE

Beaufort Number	Category	Wind Speed (mph)	Results
0	Calm	Under 1	Smoke rises vertically
1	Light Air	1 to 3	Smoke drift shows wind direction
2	Light Breeze	4 to 7	Wind is felt on face; leaves rustle, vanes move
3	Gentle Breeze	8 to 12	A light flag extends
4	Moderate Breeze	13 to 18	A small branch moves
5	Fresh Breeze	19 to 24	A small tree sways
6	Strong Breeze	25 to 31	Large branches move; umbrellas out of of control
7	Moderate Gale	32 to 38	Whole trees move
8	Fresh Gale	39 to 46	Twigs break off trees
9	Strong Gale	47 to 54	Branches break
10	Whole Gale	55 to 63	Some trees uprooted
11	Storm	64 to 73	Widespread damage occurs
12	Hurricane	74 to 136	Severe destruction

For the class

- 1 piece of white fabric, 10 x 15 cm (4 x 6 in)
- 1 piece of stiff tagboard, 5 x 18 cm (2 x 7 in)
- 1 stapler (or more)
- 1 sheet of newsprint or poster board
- 1 Post-it™ note for Weather Calendar
- 1 set of 11 weather stamps
- 1 stamp pad
- 1 date stamp
- Weather Calendar

Preparation

1. Make one copy of **Student Instructions for Making a Wind Flag,** on pg. 47, and **Record Sheet 4-A: Wind Data Graph,** on pg. 48, for each student.

2. Fold the 30 pieces of stiff tagboard in half lengthwise.

3. Using the tagboard and white fabric, make a sample flag to show the class. The student instructions show how to make the flag.

4. Using the newsprint or poster board, reproduce Figure 4-2 to create a large poster.

Figure 4-2

Class scale for
estimating wind
intensity

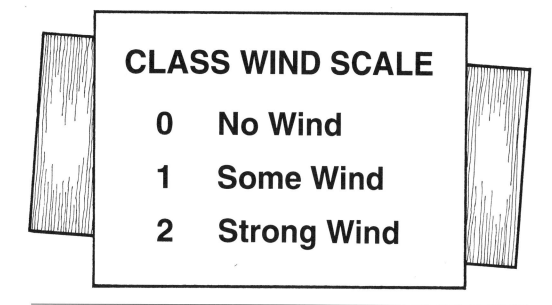

CLASS WIND SCALE

0   No Wind

1   Some Wind

2   Strong Wind

5. For this lesson, you will take the class outside to observe the school flag. If your school or a nearby building does not have a flagpole, bring a large flag or banner to school and arrange for it to be put up outdoors in a place it can stay for the rest of the unit.

Procedure

1. Ask students to describe the wind. Can they hear it? Can they feel it? Can they see it? Can they see the objects that the wind is blowing? How do they know when the wind is blowing only a little or very hard? Figure 4-3 illustrates words your students might use to describe the wind.

Figure 4-3

Students describe
the wind

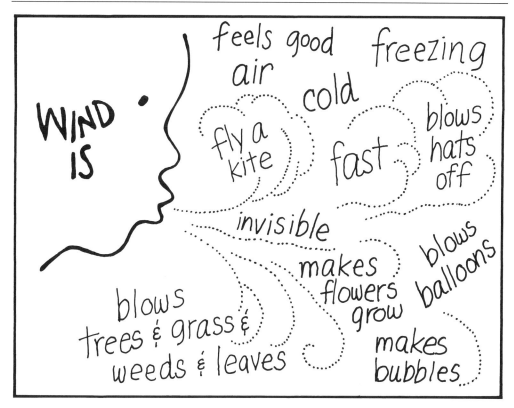

2. Talk with students about how meteorologists use observations of objects blowing in the wind to help them describe how hard or fast it is blowing. One way they do this is to observe what happens to a flag in the wind. Explain to your students that they, like meteorologists, can use the movement of a flag for estimating the speed of the wind.

3. Introduce students to the idea of using a number to describe three wind conditions: 0 for no wind, 1 for some wind, and 2 for strong wind. Display the poster of the wind scale and have students discuss what they understand that the numbers represent. Make sure that the class has a general grasp of this scale before going outside.

4. Take the class outside to the flagpole to observe the effect of the wind on the flag. Ask students to use the wind scale to estimate the wind speed by holding up zero, one, or two fingers, as shown in Figure 4-4.

5. After you return to the classroom, have students discuss what they observed outdoors. When the class agrees on the speed of the wind and its numerical value according to their wind scale, put this information on the Weather Calendar. Have one student select the wind stamp that the class decided on and stamp the Post-it™ note that shows today's weather on the Weather Calendar. Have another student write the corresponding wind scale number beneath the stamp.

6. Show students the flag that you made and let them know that they will now make their own flags to help them observe and record the wind's speed. Explain that they can work on their own or with a partner.

7. Distribute the materials needed for the flag along with a copy of **Student Instructions for Making a Wind Flag.** Review the instructions with the class.

Safety Tip

You will need to supervise students' use of the stapler.

Management Tip: Students will find it easier to decorate their flags after assembling them. This will assure that none of the decoration is hidden when they staple the fabrics to the tagboard.

8. When students have finished their flags, ask volunteers to demonstrate the wind scale by blowing on their flags with varying degrees of intensity.

Final Activities

1. Distribute one copy of **Record Sheet 4-A: Wind Data Graph** to each student. Have them record today's wind speed on the graph by putting a large letter "X" in the appropriate box. Instruct students to keep these sheets, since they will use them again.

2. Over the next six days, have students use their wind flags and the school flag as references for estimating wind speed. They record the wind speed on their graphs each day. At the end of the week, ask students to discuss and respond to the questions below the graph on the record sheet.

3. Make sure that students include observations of wind on the daily Weather Calendar.

Figure 4-4

Using the class wind scale

| 0 | 1 | 2 |
| No Wind | Some Wind | Strong Wind |

Extensions

ART

1. Put a small amount of liquid tempera on a piece of art paper. Have students use a straw to blow gently on the tempera to create a picture. How does the amount of "wind" created affect the picture?

LANGUAGE ARTS

2. Read a book about wind, such as *The Wind Blew*, by Pat Hutchins. Have students make pictures of an object blowing in the wind. Then ask them to write captions for their pictures. Put the pictures together in a class book.

LANGUAGE ARTS

3. Read a book about kites, such as *Gilberto and the Wind*, by Marie Hall Ets. Then have a "Kite Day," when students can bring in homemade or ready-made kites to fly. Challenge students to identify the best wind for flying kites. Discuss whether different types of kites need different amounts of wind.

ART   **SOCIAL ST**

4. Have students make pinwheels, wind socks, or weather vanes. If students make weather vanes, use their observations of the vanes' movement in the wind to help them learn the compass directions, north, south, east, and west.

Assessment   *Observational Guidelines*

In this lesson your students use a tool to estimate wind speed, and they begin recording their data on a graph. As you observe them during the lesson, ask yourself the following questions:

- How do students describe the wind?

- Do students describe the speed of the wind?

- Do students understand the concept of the wind scale?

- Are students simulating different wind strengths when they blow on their wind flags?

- How do students use the data on the wind graph to answer the questions on the record sheet?

- Do students recognize from looking at the data on their wind graph that wind speed can change from day to day?

Student Instructions for Making a Wind Flag

1. Insert the fabric near the top of the tagboard pole.

2. Fold the tagboard over the fabric.

3. Staple the tagboard in three places.

4. Decorate your flag and write your name on it.

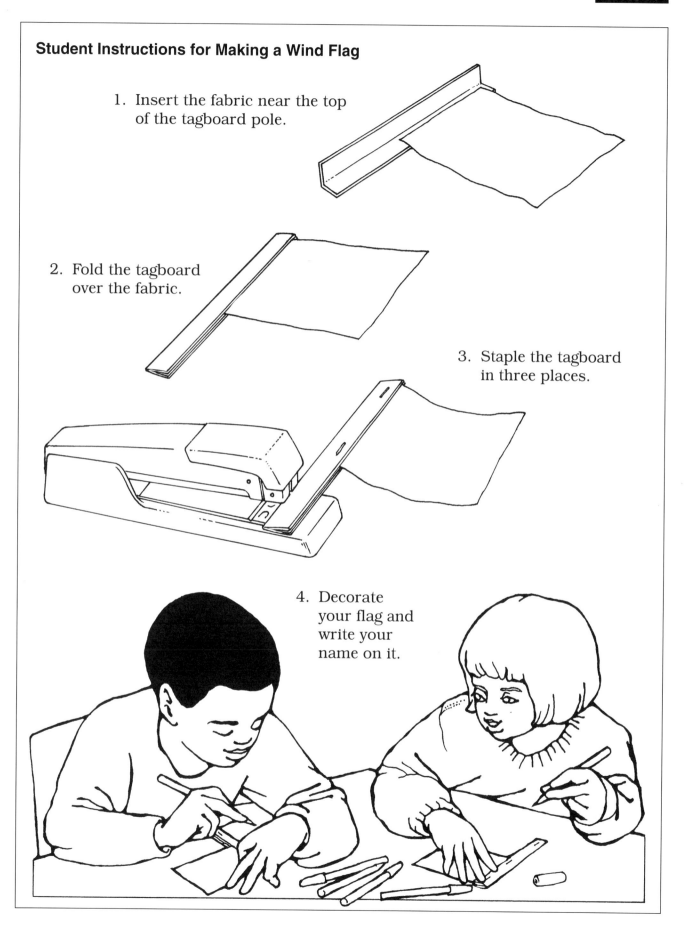

Record Sheet 4-A

Name: ------------------------------------

Date: ------------------------------------

Wind Data Graph

Wind Scale

	Sunday	Monday	Tuesday	Wednesday	Thursday	Friday	Saturday
2 Strong Wind							
1 Some Wind							
0 No Wind							

Days of the Week

1. Which day had the most wind?

_____

2. Which day had the least wind?

_____

3. Which day would have been good for kite flying?

_____

Reading a Thermometer

Overview and Objectives

This is the first of three lessons in which students explore temperature and are introduced to the tool for measuring temperature—the thermometer. Students use real thermometers to discover how a thermometer reacts to temperature and a model thermometer to learn to read the scale. As they practice reading this scale, they begin to see that the higher numbers on the scale correspond with hotter temperatures and the lower numbers correspond with colder temperatures.

- Students observe and discuss thermometers as tools that measure temperature.
- Students read the numbers on the thermometer scale.
- Students relate the numbers on the scale to hotter or colder temperatures.
- Students observe and record cloud cover, precipitation, and wind on the Weather Calendar.

Background

Temperature is most commonly measured using one of two scales: Celsius or Fahrenheit. Although the Celsius scale is used in most countries, the Fahrenheit scale is generally used in the United States. (Appendix A: The Development of the Fahrenheit and Celsius Scales provides background information on the history and use of the two scales.)

The *Weather* unit focuses on the Fahrenheit scale because of American students' greater familiarity with it. They most often hear temperatures given in Fahrenheit degrees on television and radio weather reports and in other situations in their daily lives. But because students are learning to use measurement scales in this unit, they should be aware that there is another scale commonly used for measuring temperature. At some time during the course of the unit, you can simply let them know that there are two scales—Fahrenheit, which they are learning, and another one, called the Celsius scale.

The scale on the thermometers in the *Weather* unit is designed to be age-appropriate for first-graders. Young children cannot visually track the alternating progression of numbers printed on standard Fahrenheit thermometer scales. For this reason, the numbers on the thermometers in this unit appear only on the left-hand side of the tube.

Young students can read the Fahrenheit scale, but it takes a lot of practice before they are comfortable doing so because it requires counting by twos, which is a skill they will need to develop. When students are practicing counting by twos on the thermometer scale, have them start at zero. Extension 3, on pg. 55, outlines activities that will help them practice and apply the important mathematical skill of counting by twos.

Keep in mind that for many students this unit will be an introduction to reading thermometers. What is important is that they develop an understanding of what a thermometer does, how it works, and why it is useful for them to be able to read it. A reasonable goal is for first-grade students to read and report temperature to the nearest 10. However, you will still want to work with your students to improve their ability to read temperature in increments of 2.

Materials

For each student

- 1 copy of **Record Sheet 5-A: Reading the Temperature**
- 1 copy of the blackline master **Thermometers in Our World**
- 1 thermometer
- 1 red crayon

For the class

- 1 copy of the blackline master **Large Model Fahrenheit Thermometer**
- 1 poster board, 29 x 73.5 cm (11½ x 29 in)
- 1 hole punch
- 1 white shoelace, 142 cm (56 in) long
- 1 red marker
- 1 thermometer
- 1 pair of scissors
- 1 meter stick or yardstick (optional)
- Tape and glue

Preparation

1. Make one copy of the blackline master **Thermometers in Our World,** on pg. 58, for each student.

2. Make one copy of **Record Sheet 5-A: Reading the Temperature,** on pg. 57, for each student.

3. Make a large model thermometer as shown in Figure 5-1. (Appendix B contains the blackline master for a large model Celsius thermometer.)

Procedure

1. Ask the class what they know about thermometers. You might want to use the following questions to help guide the discussion:

    - Where have you seen thermometers before?

    - What does a thermometer tell you?

    - What do you think the numbers on a thermometer mean?

2. Distribute one copy of **Thermometers in Our World** to each student. Encourage students to continue telling you what they know about thermometers by using the illustrations of different thermometers as a reference.

3. Ask students to brainstorm words that describe temperature. Then ask them which of these words describe how they feel when they go outside in the winter, spring, summer, or fall.

4. Distribute thermometers to the students. Allow a few minutes for them to observe these new tools. Invite them to describe their observations.

Figure 5-1

Instructions for making a large model thermometer

1. Make a copy of the blackline master Large Model Fahrenheit Thermometer, on pgs. 59, 60, and 61. Trim the top and bottom of the middle section.

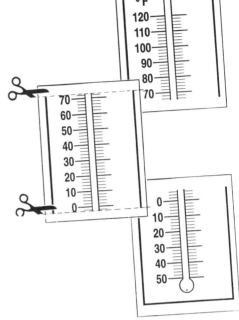

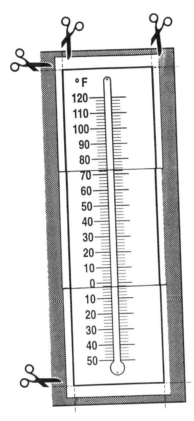

2. Tape the three sections together so that the middle section overlaps the top and bottom sections, forming a complete thermometer. Glue the thermometer to the poster board. Then, cut it out along the heavy black outline. If you want to laminate the thermometer, do so at this point.

3. Punch holes at the top and bottom of the thermometer tube where indicated. Fold a 142-cm (56-in) shoelace in half. Color one half with a red marker. (Color both sides of this half.) Slide the ends of the shoelace through the holes, making sure the red half is at the bottom. Tie two knots in each end of the shoelace.

4. To make the thermometer backing stiffer, attach a meter stick or yardstick at the back with tape, glue, or thumbtacks. Position the stick to the left or right of the "thermometer tube" to allow free movement of the shoelace.

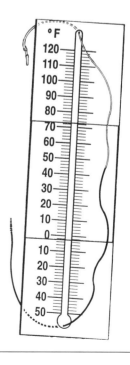

> **Safety Tip**
>
> The liquid in the glass tube of the thermometer is nontoxic and therefore poses no safety problem. Tell students to handle the thermometers with care, however, because the glass tube can break or become separated from the backing. Tell them that if a thermometer should happen to break, they must let you know immediately. You would need to clean up the broken glass.

5. Ask students to gently place their thumbs on the red bulb at the bottom of the thermometer. Ask them to describe what they observe and why they think the fluid is moving.

6. Let students know that the red fluid in the thermometer tube is sensitive to temperature and that it moves up when it gets warmer and down when it gets cooler.

7. Collect the thermometers.

8. Hold up the large model thermometer and ask students what they know about the numbers on the scale (see Figure 5-2).

9. Explain that each line on the scale stands for two numbers, even though the numbers are not all written on the scale. Point out that only the tens are written on the scale.

10. Help the class count out loud by tens from 0 to 120 and then back to 0 as you point to the numbers on the large model thermometer.

11. Explain that the numbers below zero are used to show temperatures that are very cold.

12. Direct students to look at the lines between the tens, reminding them that each line stands for two numbers. Help them count by twos from 0 to 20 and back to 0 as you point to the lines on the large model thermometer.

13. Move the shoelace to different temperatures and give children the opportunity to read each temperature. You may want to start with only temperatures on the tens lines before practicing with numbers between these lines.

14. Vary your guided practice by allowing students to take turns setting the model thermometer and calling on others to read it. Also, ask a student to name a temperature for you to show on the model thermometer.

Final Activities

1. Distribute one red crayon and one copy of **Record Sheet 5-A: Reading the Temperature** to each student.

2. Direct students' attention to the dark mark on the thermometer scale at 80°F. (On the Celsius thermometer, the dark mark is at 30°C.) Have them color the thermometer tube from the bulb to this dark mark with their red crayons.

3. Ask each student to write his or her response to the two questions on the record sheet. Explain to students that "°F" means "degrees Fahrenheit."

4. Have each student draw a picture in the space below the second question on the record sheet. The picture should show what the student would wear (for example, a bathing suit) or an activity (swimming) that he or she might take part in if the weather today was the temperature that the thermometer on the record sheet shows.

5. Save Record Sheet 5-A for use in the Final Assessments (Assessment 4).

Figure 5-2

*Reading a
Fahrenheit
thermometer*

Extensions

SCIENCE

SOCIAL STUDIES

MATHEMATICS

1. Introduce the concept of freezing. Encourage students to share experiences they have had making ice cubes. Have them describe the sequence of what they think happens when water is put in the freezer overnight.

2. Use a map to show students places that sometimes have subzero temperatures, such as Alaska, the northern Rocky Mountains, or the Great Plains states. Also point out places that we often think of as being extremely hot, such as Texas or the Sahara.

3. Using a Fahrenheit scale involves counting by twos, or "skip counting." This is an opportunity for students to experience a practical application of an important mathematical skill. The ideas below can help them practice counting by twos.

    ■ As students line up for lunch or recess, have them count off, with the even-numbered students saying their numbers louder.

    ■ Have the class do this exercise: "How many mittens (or shoes) do we need for everyone to have a pair? We have two hands (or feet), so let's count by twos."

■ Have students break sticks of ten Unifix Cubes™ into sets of two and count up to ten by twos.

■ Place clothespins on the even numbers of a large number line. Have students practice reading the numbers beneath the clothespins. One way to do this is to have students "snap" the odd numbers with their fingers and say the even numbers.

Assessment

Lessons 5, 6, and 7 focus on thermometers and temperature. In Lesson 7, students will begin recording the daily temperature on the Weather Calendar and on a Temperature Graph.

Observational Guidelines

As you observe your students working with model and real thermometers over the next few lessons, use the following questions as guidelines to help you assess their understanding.

■ Do students discuss how the red fluid reacts to temperature changes?

■ Do students mention various types of thermometers during the class discussion?

■ Are students beginning to be able to read the temperature set on the large model thermometer and on their own model thermometers to the nearest 10? To the nearest 2?

■ Do students identify clothes or activities that are appropriate for different temperatures?

■ Do students understand why the outside temperature tells them more about the weather than the inside temperature?

Using Record Sheets for Assessment

Look at each student's completed copy of **Record Sheet 5-A** and **Record Sheet 6-A.**

■ Did the student record the temperature shown on the thermometer to the nearest 10? To the nearest 2?

■ Does the student's drawing correlate with the temperature shown on the thermometer?

Save both record sheets. In Final Assessment 4 (on pg. 160), students are asked to complete record sheets similar to 5-A and 6-A. A comparison of the two pairs of record sheets will help you assess your students' growth in reading and recording temperatures and in their ability to relate the specific temperatures on the record sheets to appropriate activities or clothing.

Using the Temperature Graph for Assessment

As students record the daily temperature on the graph, ask the following questions:

■ Do students record temperatures on the graph correctly?

■ Do students recognize that the graph shows temperatures over a long period of time?

■ When discussing the graph, do students seem to recognize that the temperature changes?

Record Sheet 5-A

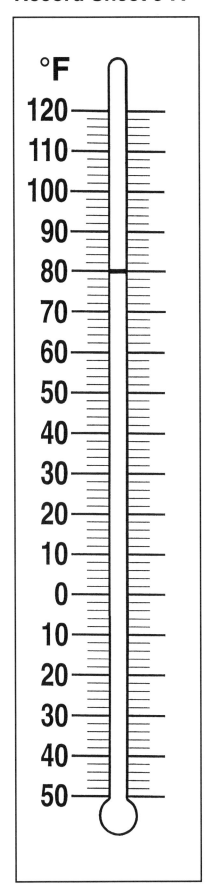

Name: _____

Date: _____

Reading the Temperature

What is the temperature? _ _ _ _ _ _ _ _ _ °F

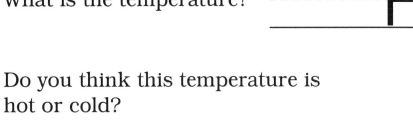

Do you think this temperature is
hot or cold?

_____

_____

Thermometers in Our World

Aquarium Thermometer

Fever Thermometer

Engine Temperature Gauge

Bank Thermometer

Swimming Pool Thermometer

Meat Thermometer

Window Thermometer

Thermostat Thermometer

Large Model Fahrenheit Thermometer (top section)

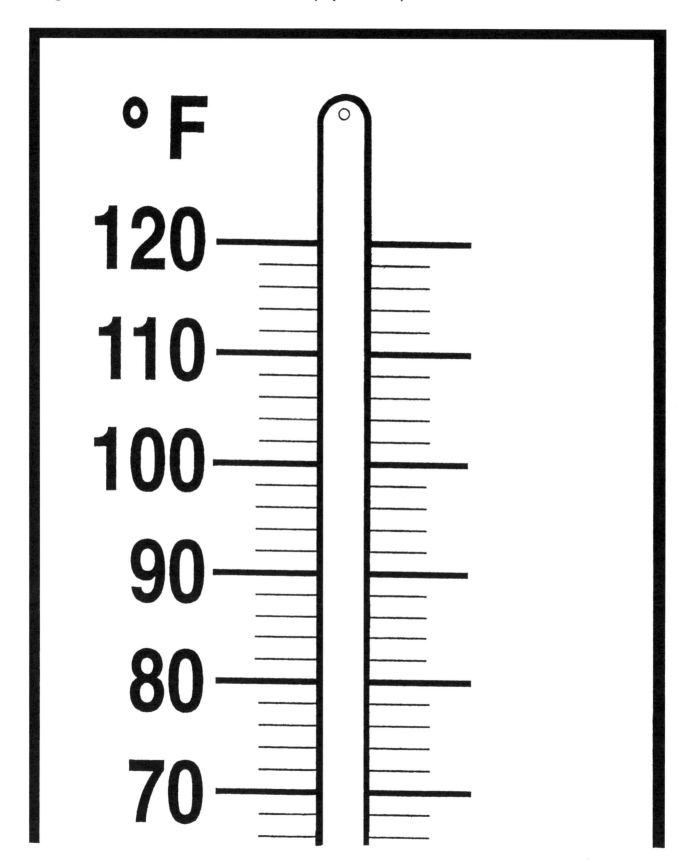

Large Model Fahrenheit Thermometer (middle section)

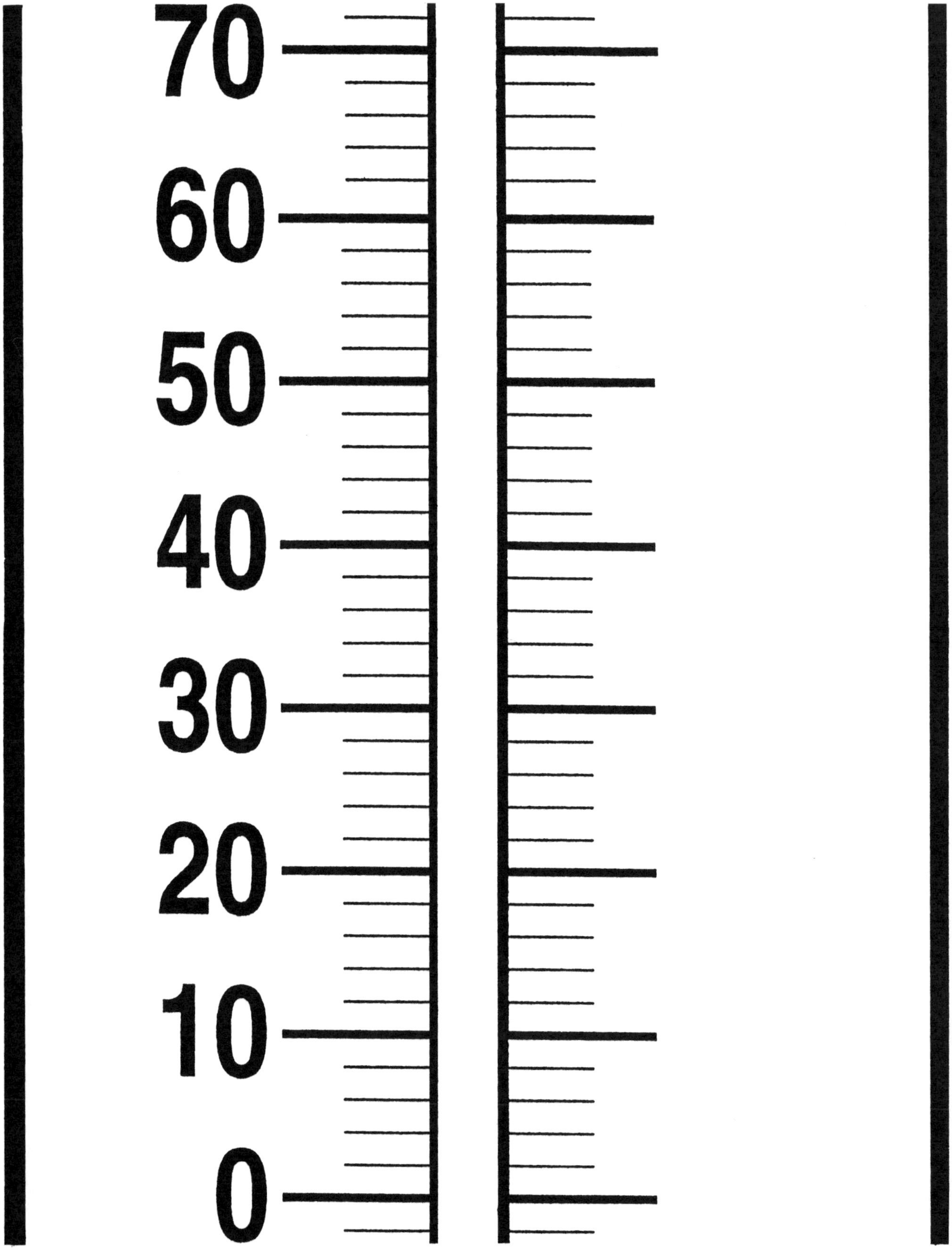

70

60

50

40

30

20

10

0

Large Model Fahrenheit Thermometer (bottom section)

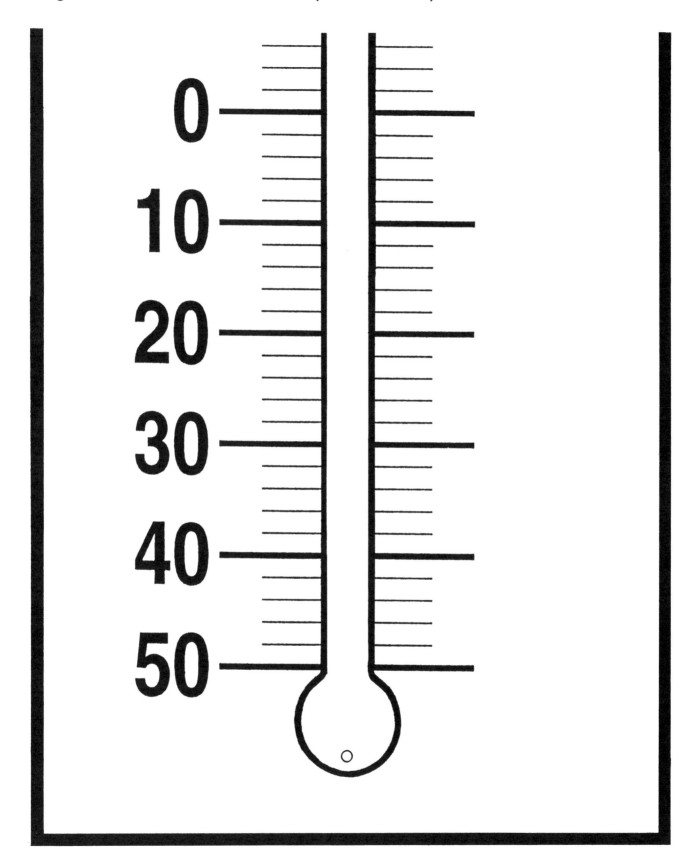

Making a Model Thermometer

Overview and Objectives

Lesson 5 introduced students to an important new weather feature, temperature, and to a scientific measuring tool, the Fahrenheit thermometer. In this lesson they will continue developing the skill of reading the thermometer scale and relating the numbers on the scale to hotter or colder temperatures. So that they can gain practice reading many different temperatures, students make model thermometers whose temperature they can adjust themselves. Practicing this skill prepares them for the next lesson, when they will be using real thermometers to measure temperature.

■ Students read temperatures on model thermometers.

■ Students read and record the temperature shown on an illustration of a thermometer.

■ Students relate a specific temperature to appropriate activities and clothing.

■ Students observe, discuss, and record today's weather on the Weather Calendar.

Background

This lesson is a continuation of the work begun in Lesson 5. It gives students more time to practice reading the Fahrenheit scale. During practice sessions, you will want to consider pairing a student who has been successful reading the thermometer with a student who finds it more difficult. Most students would probably also benefit from continuing to practice counting by twos and tens.

Materials

For each student

  1 copy of **Student Instructions for Making a Model Thermometer**
  1 copy of **Record Sheet 6-A: What Is the Temperature?**
  1 backing for small model thermometer
  1 white shoelace, 61 cm (24 in) long
  1 red crayon
  1 pencil

For the class

  1 hole punch
  1 large model thermometer (from Lesson 5)
  1 backing for small model thermometer
  1 white shoelace, 61 cm (24 in) long
  1 red crayon

Preparation

1. Make one copy of **Student Instructions for Making a Model Thermometer,** found on pg. 67, for each student.

2. For each student, make one copy of **Record Sheet 6-A: What Is the Temperature?,** on pg. 68.

3. Using the shoelace, small thermometer backing, and red crayon, make one model thermometer according to the student instructions.

4. Using the hole punch, make a hole at the top and bottom of the scale on each of the 30 thermometer backings. The shoelace will go through these holes and will represent the tube.

Procedure

1. Ask students to share what they learned about thermometers in Lesson 5.

2. Show students the small model thermometer and explain that they will each make their own.

3. Distribute student instructions and outline the steps for making the model thermometer.

4. Then distribute the materials students need (thermometer backing, shoelace, red crayon, pencil), and allow time for them to assemble the model thermometers. Ask them to write their name in pencil on the back of their model thermometers.

Management Tip: Make sure students thread the shoestring with the red section in the lower half of the thermometer backing. You may also need to help students tie the knots at the ends of the shoelace.

5. After the model thermometers are assembled, provide time for students to practice setting them at certain temperatures. Demonstrate this on the large model thermometer, and have students set their own small thermometers at the same temperature. Depending on your students' progress, you may want to focus first on temperatures that are in increments of 10 degrees before moving to increments of 2 degrees.

6. After you have asked students to set their model thermometers at various temperatures, have individual students select temperatures for the rest of the class to set.

7. For additional practice, have students work in pairs: one student can set a temperature while the other reads it. (See Figure 6-1.)

Final Activities

1. Distribute to each student a red crayon and one copy of **Record Sheet 6-A: What Is the Temperature?**

2. Direct students' attention to the dark mark on the thermometer scale at 30°F. (Note that the mark is at 30°F, not 32°F, because the intent is to show a "cold" temperature, not freezing. On the Celsius version of the record sheet, the dark mark is at 0°C.) Have students color the thermometer tube from the bulb to this dark mark with the red crayon.

3. Ask each student to write responses to the two questions on Record Sheet 6-A. Remind them that "°F" means degrees Fahrenheit.

4. Ask students to draw a picture in the space below the second question on the record sheet. The picture should show what the child would wear (for example, mittens and a hat) or an activity that he or she would do (perhaps

Figure 6-1

Reading the model thermometer

building a snowman) if the temperature was what the thermometer on the record sheet shows.

5. Save Record Sheet 6-A for use in the Final Assessments (Assessment 4).

Extensions

MATHEMATICS

1. Play a guessing game with temperature. Have one student set a secret temperature on either the large or the small model thermometer. Then ask other students to try to guess it by asking "yes-or-no" questions. For example, the secret temperature is 30°F. (For Celsius, change the temperatures in this example.)

Question:	Is it a cold temperature?
Answer:	Yes.
Question:	Is it below 20°F?
Answer:	No.
Question:	Is it hotter than 25°F?
Answer:	Yes.

SCIENCE

2. Make an overhead transparency of the Fahrenheit thermometer illustrated on Record Sheet 6-A. Using thin strips of paper, set different temperatures on the overhead and have students practice reading the temperatures.

LANGUAGE ARTS

3. In their journals, have students first write similes by filling in the blanks in the examples below and then draw pictures to illustrate each sentence.

    [For example: A snowball] is as cold as an ice cube.

    [For example: The stove] is as hot as a fire.

LANGUAGE ARTS

4. Read a book such as *Temperature and You,* by Betsy and Giulio Maestro.

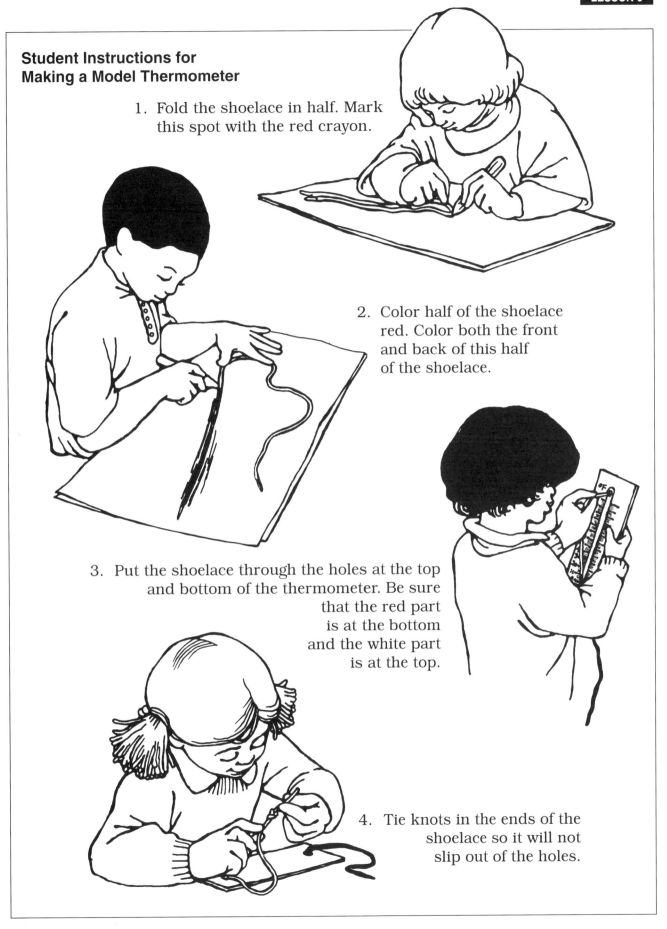

**Student Instructions for
Making a Model Thermometer**

1. Fold the shoelace in half. Mark this spot with the red crayon.

2. Color half of the shoelace red. Color both the front and back of this half of the shoelace.

3. Put the shoelace through the holes at the top and bottom of the thermometer. Be sure that the red part is at the bottom and the white part is at the top.

4. Tie knots in the ends of the shoelace so it will not slip out of the holes.

Record Sheet 6-A

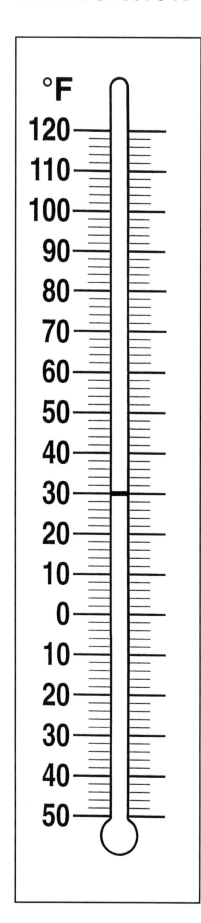

Name: -

Date: -

What Is the Temperature?

What is the temperature? - - - - - - - - °F

Do you think this temperature is
hot or cold?

- -

Comparing Inside and Outside Temperatures

Overview and Objectives

Students continue their exploration of temperature and thermometers by recording and comparing actual temperatures in the classroom and outside. A class discussion helps students recognize that it is the outside temperature that gives them information about the weather. Students begin to use their second long-term data collection tool, the Temperature Graph, to record the daily temperature. They will continue recording temperature on the graph throughout the rest of the unit.

■ Students read the scale on a real thermometer.

■ Students measure, record, and compare the temperatures in the classroom and outside.

■ The class compiles temperature data on a graph.

■ Students continue to collect weather data and record it on the Weather Calendar.

Background

Your students will continue to need practice time as they learn to read the Fahrenheit scale. Some students may not master actually reading the thermometer, but as they practice this skill in class, most will develop the understanding that thermometers measure temperature.

The Fahrenheit thermometers provided with the *Weather* unit are guaranteed to be accurate within 2 degrees. Keep this in mind in case students find slightly differing temperatures when the whole class is reading a temperature for the same environment.

In this lesson, students begin to record the daily temperature on a graph. At the end of the *Weather* unit, you will use this Temperature Graph to discuss variations in temperature from day to day, as well as from season to season.

Materials

For each student

1 copy of **Record Sheet 7-A: Recording the Temperature Inside**
1 copy of **Record Sheet 7-B: Recording the Temperature Outside**
1 thermometer
1 red crayon

For the class

3 sheets of large graph paper with 2.5-cm (1-in) squares
1 red marker
Weather Calendar
Tape

Preparation

1. Make one copy of **Record Sheet 7-A** and **Record Sheet 7-B,** on pgs. 76 and 77, for each student.

2. Use one large sheet of graph paper to make the Temperature Graph, as illustrated in Figure 7-1. Tape the graph on a wall so that it is within easy reach for the students. Use the other two sheets of graph paper, as needed, to maintain the Temperature Graph for the rest of the unit.

3. Establish a system for having students measure and record the temperature. The box entitled **"Recording the Daily Temperature,"** on pg. 73, suggests ways to do this.

Figure 7-1

An example of the Temperature Graph

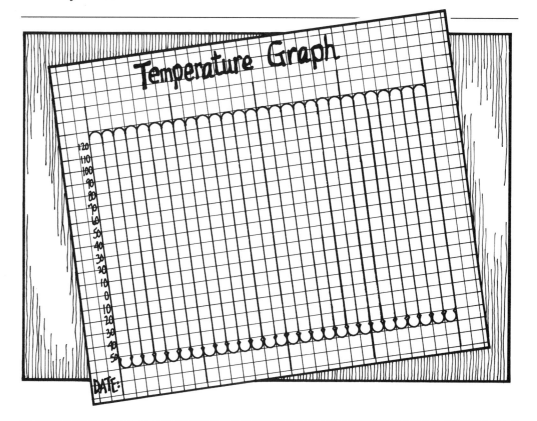

Recording the Daily Temperature

You may want to consider the following options as you make assignments for measuring and recording the daily temperature.

■ Have the daily weather recorders in your class assume the related responsibility of measuring and recording the daily temperature on the Temperature Graph.

■ Assign different students each day to measure and record the temperature on the graph.

■ Record the daily temperature on the Weather Calendar as well as on the Temperature Graph. Make sure students label their temperatures "°F."

■ Record the temperature at the same time each day, noting the time on the Temperature Graph or the Weather Calendar or both.

■ Assign certain students to take home a thermometer over weekends and on holidays to measure the temperature. Send home copies of **Record Sheet 7-B** with these students and have them record the temperatures on the sheets.

■ Consider obtaining a window thermometer to place outside your classroom window if measuring the temperature outside each day creates a supervision problem. Make sure the thermometer is placed in a shaded location, not in direct sunlight.

Procedure

1. Ask students to think about the temperature inside the classroom and the temperature outside today. Do they think the two are the same or different? Is it warmer outside than it is inside today, or colder? How could they find out?

2. Distribute the thermometers. Have students place their thumbs gently on the bulbs of their thermometers. After about one minute, ask them to read the temperature.

Safety Tip

Remind students to handle the thermometers with care and to tell you immediately if a thermometer tube breaks.

---

3. Ask students what they think the thermometer is measuring. End this discussion by reminding them that because the bulb is sensitive to their touch, they need to be careful not to touch it when they are measuring inside and outside temperatures.

4. Distribute a red crayon and a copy of **Record Sheet 7-A: Recording the Temperature Inside** to each student. Have students place their thermometers next to their record sheets and wait two minutes. Then ask them to read the temperature, record it on Record Sheet 7-A, and color the thermometer tube. Remind them to write "°F" after the temperature.

5. Have students share their results. Depending on the results they find, you may need to explain to them that these student Fahrenheit thermometers can vary by 2 degrees.

6. Take the class outside. Students need to take along their thermometers, **Record Sheet 7-B: Recording the Temperature Outside,** and their red crayons. Have them measure and record the outside temperature. Make sure that they do not place the thermometers in direct sunlight.

7. Back in the classroom, have students look at Record Sheets 7-A and 7-B side by side. Have them compare the two temperatures and help them recognize that only the outside temperature tells them what the weather is like. Ask them questions such as the following:

- Are these temperatures the same?

- Which is hotter? Which is colder?

- Why do you think the inside temperature is lower (or higher)?

- Which temperature tells us more about today's weather? Why?

Final Activities

1. Show students the Temperature Graph. Explain that it, like the Weather Calendar, is a useful long-term recording tool from which they can learn more about temperature.

2. Review the Temperature Graph with students, showing them that it has the Fahrenheit scale and that each column represents one thermometer.

3. Using a red crayon, color in the graph to show today's temperature, as demonstrated in Figure 7-2. Let students know that filling in the Temperature Graph will now be part of their daily recording of weather data.

Figure 7-2

Filling in the Temperature Graph

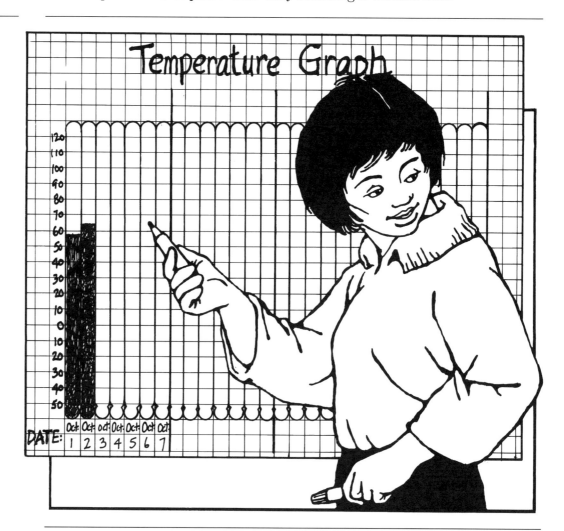

Extensions

SCIENCE

SCIENCE

SCIENCE

SCIENCE

1. Challenge students to locate the thermostat in their homes and to find out how the temperature is regulated. Ask them to find out how their homes are heated and cooled.

2. Invite the school nurse or a health care professional to talk with the class about how to take body temperature and about normal body temperature ranges. Ask the visitor to bring samples of the newer types of thermometer: plastic forehead strips or digital thermometers.

3. Ask the school custodian to take your class on a tour of the school's heating and air conditioning system. Before the tour, have students brainstorm questions they would like to ask.

4. Have students measure and record the temperature at different times of day, discussing why they think these temperatures differ.

Record Sheet 7-A

Name: ----------------------------------

Date: ----------------------------------

Recording the Temperature Inside

The temperature inside is ------------- .

Color this temperature on the thermometer.

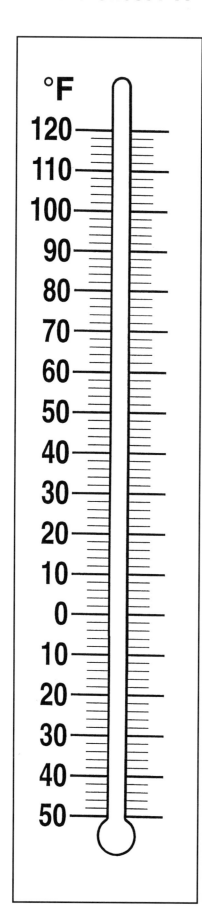

°F

120
110
100
90
80
70
60
50
40
30
20
10
0
10
20
30
40
50

Record Sheet 7-B

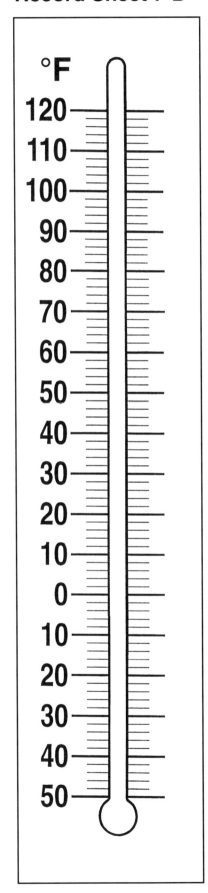

Name: ------------------------------------

Date: ------------------------------------

Recording the Temperature Outside

The temperature outside is ----------- .

Color this temperature on the thermometer.

Measuring Water Temperature

Overview and Objectives

Lessons 5, 6, and 7 introduced students to the thermometer as a measurement tool for temperature. Using both real and model thermometers, they practiced reading the thermometer scale. This lesson reinforces those experiences and provides an opportunity for students to apply what they learned as they conduct an experiment that involves water of different temperatures. The activity also serves as an embedded assessment of students' growth in learning to read and record temperature.

- Students measure the temperatures of hot and cold water.

- Students conduct an experiment and discuss the results.

- Students record their data on a graph.

Background

In this lesson, students measure and record the temperature of hot and cold water and then conduct an experiment to discover what happens when hot and cold water are mixed. This activity also serves as an embedded assessment. As students conduct the experiment, you can observe them and assess their progress and growth in learning to read and record temperatures, a skill they have been practicing for the last few lessons.

As you observe your students, look for evidence of whether they are able to work with the thermometers effectively and whether they read and record the temperatures correctly. The Assessment section at the end of this lesson provides more specific observational guidelines to help you assess your students' skills.

Materials

For each student

  1   copy of **Record Sheet 8-A: Graphing Water Temperature**
  1   thermometer
  1   red crayon

For every three students

  1   copy of the three-page blackline master **Water Place Mats**
  3   large plastic cups, 473 ml (16 oz)
  1   small plastic cup, 118 ml (4 oz)

For the class

1 plastic pail of hot water, 3.8 liters (1 gal)
1 plastic pail of cold water, 3.8 liters (1 gal)
1 thermometer
1 sheet of newsprint
Marker
Paper towels or sponges

Preparation

1. Make one copy of **Record Sheet 8-A: Graphing Water Temperature,** on pg. 85, for each student.

2. For each group of three students, make one copy of the three-page blackline master **Water Place Mats,** on pgs. 86, 87 and 88. (You may want to have extra copies available in case students get them wet.)

3. Divide the class into working groups of three students each.

4. On the sheet of newsprint, make a chart entitled "The Water-Mixing Experiment," like the one illustrated in Figure 8-1. In the first column, write the names or initials of the students in each group.

5. Fill one plastic pail with hot water that is between 100°F and 120°F (between 35°C and 50°C). Fill the other pail with cold water. (You will want to locate a convenient source of hot water, such as the school cafeteria, before the lesson begins.)

> **Safety Tip**
>
> The hot water temperature *should not exceed* 120°F (50°C). Water that is hotter can melt the plastic cups and might burn the children.

6. Set up a distribution center where students can collect the hot and cold water and the cups. Figure 8-2 illustrates one way to arrange the materials so that several students can easily have access to them at once.

Procedure

1. Hold up two large plastic cups of water, one hot and one cold. Ask students how they can find out which is hot and which is cold. They may suggest putting their fingers in the water or using a thermometer.

2. Let students know that they will measure the temperatures of hot and cold water and will then conduct an experiment to investigate what happens to the water temperature when the hot and cold water are mixed.

3. Assign one student in each group to be responsible for the cold water, one for the hot water, and one for the mixed water.

4. Distribute one set of the **Water Place Mats,** three thermometers, and red crayons to each group.

> **Safety Tip**
>
> Remind students to handle the thermometers with care and to tell you immediately if a thermometer tube breaks.

Figure 8-1

A chart for recording experiment results

THE WATER-MIXING EXPERIMENT

Group	Cups COLD Water	Cups HOT Water	Mixed Water Temperature

5. Direct the students responsible for the cold water to go to the distribution center. There they should measure two small cups of cold water, pouring them into a large plastic cup.

6. Have each student responsible for cold water return to his or her group and place the cup on the circle on the Cold Water Place Mat (see Figure 8-3). Then have that student put the thermometer into the cup. As soon as the red fluid in the thermometer stops moving, he or she should record the temperature in the space provided below the circle on the place mat. Have all of the students in the group put a finger into the water to feel the temperature.

7. Have the students responsible for the hot water repeat the same basic procedure.

Management Tip: You might have students collect both the hot and the cold water (**Procedure,** Steps 6 and 7) at the same time to speed up the process, because the longer this takes, the more the hot water cools off and the cold water warms up.

Figure 8-2

A distribution center

8. Ask students in each group to look at the temperatures for the cold and hot water recorded on their place mats. Have them discuss with each other what they think will happen when they mix the hot and cold water.

9. Ask each group to decide how many small cups of cold water and hot water they want to mix together. Since the large cup will hold four small cups of water and they are using the water already at their work stations, their choices are as follows:

   ■ Two small cups of cold and one of hot

   ■ Two small cups of hot and one of cold

   ■ Two small cups of hot and two of cold

   Record the choice of each group on "The Water-Mixing Experiment" chart.

10. Have the student from each group who is responsible for the mixed water pick up one large plastic cup and one small plastic cup from the distribution center. These students do not need to get water from the distribution center, since they will be using the hot and cold water already at their tables.

11. Have the students responsible for the mixed water return to their groups and place the large empty cups on the circle on the Mixed Water Place Mats.

12. Next, have these students use the small cups to measure the hot and cold water into the large cups. Have them put the thermometers in the cups and record the temperature on the Mixed Water Place Mats.

13. Make sure each student in each group puts a finger in the cup to feel the temperature of the mixed water.

14. Ask each group to share with the class the temperature of the water they mixed. Record these temperatures on "The Water-Mixing Experiment" chart. Remember to write "°F" after each temperature.

Figure 8-3

Using the water
place mats

Figure 8-4

Feeling the water
temperature

Final Activities

1. Have students clean up by returning their thermometers to the distribution center and emptying their cups in the plastic pails. Students should keep the red crayons and the **Water Place Mats** at their desks.

2. Distribute one copy of **Record Sheet 8-A: Graphing Water Temperature** to each student. Have each student complete the graph to show the temperature of the cold water, the hot water, and the mixed water that his or her group measured.

3. Ask students to look at "The Water-Mixing Experiment" chart and the graphs as they respond to the following questions:

   ■ Did any group find the temperature of the mixed water to be hotter than the hot water?

   ■ Did any group find the temperature of the mixed water to be colder than the cold water?

   ■ Did any group find the temperature of the mixed water to be between the temperature of the cold water and that of the hot water?

   ■ Did the number of cups of hot and cold water mixed together affect the temperature?

   ■ Would they call the temperature of the mixed water cool or warm? Why?

Extensions

| SCIENCE |

| SCIENCE |

1. Have students record the temperature of various liquids at home, using, for example, tap water and rainwater.

2. Have students find the temperature of a glass of ice water. Ask them to predict and then find out what happens to the temperature of the water as the ice melts.

Assessment

Observational Guidelines

Because students apply what they have learned about thermometers as they conduct the experiment, this embedded assessment provides an opportunity for you to observe students as they work. The following questions may be helpful:

■ Do students read the temperature on the thermometer to the nearest 10? To the nearest 2?

■ Do students record this temperature on the place mats?

■ Can students record the three temperatures on their graphs?

■ Do students conclude that mixing hot and cold water produces warm or cool water?

■ Do students use the class data recorded on the "Water-Mixing Experiment" chart to help them draw their conclusions about the results of the experiment?

Record Sheet 8-A

**Graphing
Water Temperature**

Name: _____

Date: _____

°F

120
110
100
90
80
70
60
50
40
30
20
10
0
10
20
30
40
50

Cold Water   **Hot Water**   **Mixed Water**

Cold Water Place Mat

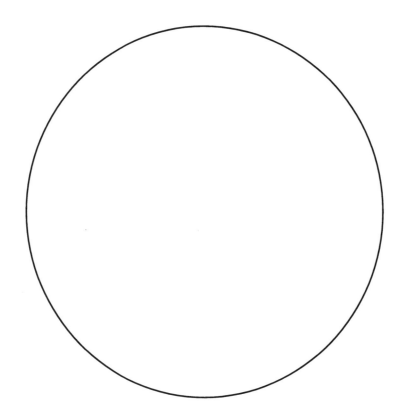

°F

_____

Hot Water Place Mat

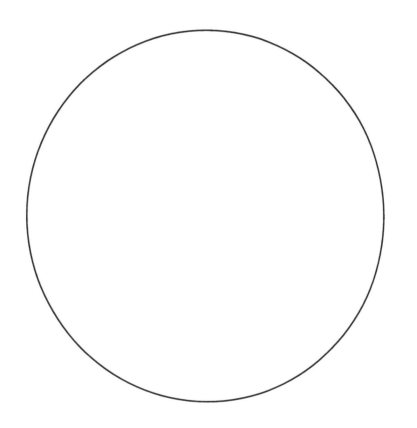

°F

_____

Mixed Water Place Mat

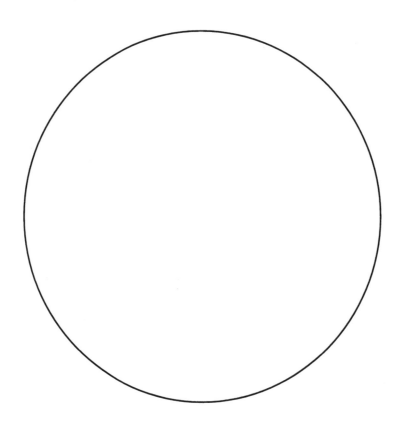

_____ °F

Experimenting with Color and Temperature

Overview and Objectives

Students have now acquired experience reading the thermometer scale and recording temperature. In this lesson they apply those skills in an experiment to investigate the effect colors can have on thermometer readings. Discussing the results of their experiment can help students determine the color of clothing they might choose to wear in specific types of weather.

- Students set up a simple experiment with thermometers.

- Students record the temperature shown on thermometers placed in black and white coverings.

- Students interpret the data.

- Students apply the results of the experiment to draw practical conclusions.

Background

A person wearing dark-colored clothing on a bright, sunny day feels hotter than a person wearing light-colored clothing. This is because dark-colored clothing absorbs sunlight, and when light energy is absorbed and retained, the clothing becomes hotter. So does the person wearing it! Light-colored clothing, however, reflects sunlight, so the light has less effect on its temperature.

In this lesson, students investigate these phenomena by conducting an experiment to observe the different effects black construction paper and white construction paper have on temperature readings. As a practical application of what they learn, students draw conclusions about the color of clothing they probably want to wear on hot, sunny days.

Clearly, the weather will have an effect on your students' success with this lesson. You will need to conduct this activity on a sunny day. Also keep in mind that factors in addition to sunlight may affect the outcome of the lesson. For example, on a very cold day, students' thermometers may register the cold ground temperature, and so the thermometers in both the white and black bags would register the same temperature.

Therefore, you will want to do the activity yourself to determine whether weather conditions are generally favorable before conducting this experiment with your students. If the weather is not suitable for doing the activity, you might want to consider simulating sunlight by placing the thermometers under a gooseneck lamp.

Materials

For each student

1   copy of **Student Instructions for Making a Thermometer Bag**
1   copy of **Record Sheet 9-A: Temperature and Color**
1   thermometer
4   pieces of transparent tape, approximately 5 cm (2 in) each

For the class

15   sheets of white construction paper, 23 x 28 cm (9 x 11 in)
15   sheets of black construction paper, 23 x 28 cm (9 x 11 in)
2   sheets of newsprint
2   markers

Preparation

1. Make a copy of **Student Instructions for Making a Thermometer Bag,** on pg. 96, and **Record Sheet 9-A: Temperature and Color,** on pg. 97, for each student.

2. Identify a sunny outside location where the students can conduct this experiment.

3. On one sheet of newsprint, make a chart called "Predicting Temperatures." On the second sheet of newsprint, create a chart with the title "Recording Temperatures." Both charts are illustrated in Figure 9-1.

Procedure

1. Talk with students about what may be a new concept for them—that the color of their clothes can affect how hot they feel when they are in direct sunlight. Encourage them to think about how they feel in either dark- or light-colored shirts or dresses on a hot, sunny day.

2. Suggest to students that one way to investigate this subject is to do an experiment using black and white paper.

3. Describe the experiment to the class. Each student will

    ■   Make either a black or a white bag

    ■   Put a thermometer in the bag

    ■   Put the bag with the thermometer in it outside in the sun

    ■   Read the temperature shown on the thermometer

    ■   Record that temperature on a record sheet

4. Distribute a copy of **Student Instructions for Making a Thermometer Bag** and a sheet of black or white construction paper to each student.

5. Demonstrate the steps for folding and taping the construction paper to make a bag as students follow the instructions. Dispense four pieces of tape to each student.

6. Show students the class chart "Predicting Temperatures." Ask them which they think will have the higher temperature—the thermometers in the black bags or the white bags. Use tally marks to record their responses on the chart.

7. Distribute thermometers and copies of **Record Sheet 9-A: Temperature and Color.** Then take the class outside to conduct the experiment.

Figure 9-1

Charts for
predicting and
recording
temperatures

Safety Tip

Remind students to handle the thermometers with care and to tell you immediately if a thermometer tube breaks.

---

8. Have students put the bags with thermometers in them in the sun for 10 minutes. During this time, ask students to think about and describe how warm or hot they feel. Help them relate this to the color of the clothes they are wearing.

Management Tip: All thermometers should be placed on the same type of surface. If they are placed on different surfaces, such as grass and concrete, the results can be significantly different.

9. After 10 minutes, ask students to slide the thermometers out of the bags just far enough so that they can read the temperature. Then have them record the temperature on Record Sheet 9-A. Remind them to write "°F" after the temperature.

Management Tip: Make sure that students touch only the backing and not the tubes as they slide the thermometers out of the bags.

Final Activities

1. Ask students to write the temperatures from their record sheets on the "Recording Temperatures" chart. Provide two markers so that two students can record temperatures at the same time.

2. Ask students to look at the data on the chart as they discuss the following questions:

   ■ Are most of the temperatures from the thermometers in the black bags higher or lower than the those from thermometers in the white bags?

   ■ Would you say that color does or does not affect temperature on the thermometer?

   ■ Why do you think so?

3. Ask students to discuss the effect of their discovery on the color of clothing they might choose to wear. Use the following questions to start the discussion:

   ■ What color T-shirt would you wear on a very hot, sunny day if you wanted to stay cool?

   ■ What color sweat shirt would you wear on a cool, sunny day if you wanted to stay warm?

Extensions

SCIENCE

MATHEMATICS

1. Challenge students to conduct the experiment in this lesson with paper bags of other colors: for example, deep purple and yellow.

2. Encourage students to think about how the weather in general affects the kinds of clothes they wear. Make a Venn diagram on which students can record the types of clothing they wear in hot and cold weather, as illustrated in Figure 9-2.

Figure 9-2

Clothes for hot and cold weather

SCIENCE

3. Have students add any new questions they may have to the list of weather questions they generated in Lesson 2. Encourage them to discuss ways they could answer some of these questions—for example, by inviting an expert to the class, visiting a local weather station, doing research, or even conducting an experiment.

Student Instructions for Making a Thermometer Bag

1. Fold the paper in half.

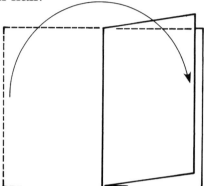

2. Fold the paper in half again.

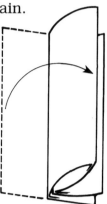

3. Unfold the paper. Now fold it from right to left at each fold so that it makes a "bag."

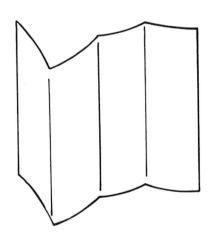

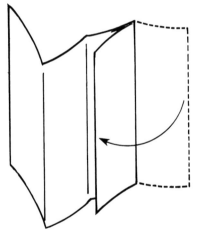

4. Put two pieces of tape on one end of the bag.

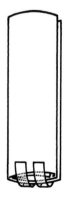

5. Put two pieces of tape on the side of the bag.

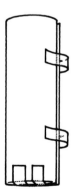

6. Write your name on the bag.

Record Sheet 9-A

Name: ------------------------------

Date: ------------------------------

Temperature and Color

The color of my thermometer bag is ------------------------------●

The temperature is ------------------------------●

Making a Rain Gauge

Overview and Objectives

So far in the unit, students have observed four weather features: cloud cover, precipitation, wind, and temperature. They have also incorporated the use of scales for estimating wind speed and measuring temperature into their daily collection of weather data. Students now begin a series of three lessons in which they focus on one form of precipitation—rain. In this lesson they construct and practice using a rain gauge, which is the third scale they will use in the unit.

■ Students construct rain gauges.

■ Students measure and record the amount of rainfall in their rain gauges.

■ The class results are recorded on a chart.

Background

There are many types of rain gauges. The simplest is a container that has straight sides and a scale attached on the outside. In this unit children use a scale based on Unifix Cubes™. (If there is not much rainfall in your area, you may want to consider using a scale with smaller divisions.) The advantage of this type of rain gauge is that young children can read the measurement on the same container in which the rain is collected.

To introduce your class to the rain gauge, a rain shower is simulated with a watering can. Later, children can collect and measure real rain as it falls naturally.

Materials

For every two students
1   copy of **Student Instructions for Making a Rain Gauge**
2   copies of **Record Sheet 10-A: Using a Rain Gauge**
2   large plastic cups, 473 ml (16 oz)
2   pieces of clear packing tape, each approximately 11 cm (4.5 in) long
2   pieces of masking tape, each approximately 10 cm (4 in) long
    Crayons

For the class
2   copies of the blackline master **Rain Gauge Scales**
1   watering can or plastic milk carton
1   sheet of newsprint
1   pair of scissors

Preparation **Management Tip:** Students will need help as they make their rain gauges. You may want to invite parent volunteers or older students from another class to help with this lesson.

1. Make one copy of **Student Instructions for Making a Rain Gauge,** on pg. 104, for every two students.

2. Make one copy of **Record Sheet 10-A: Using a Rain Gauge,** on pg. 105, for each student.

3. Make two copies of the blackline master **Rain Gauge Scales** and cut out the individual Unifix Cube™ scales that appear on them.

4. On the sheet of newsprint, make a chart entitled "Record of Rainfall." Figure 10-1 shows how to make this chart.

Figure 10-1

A sample chart for tallying rainfall data

5. If you are using a plastic carton instead of a watering can to simulate rainfall, poke small holes in the carton for sprinkling water into the rain gauges.

6. Choose a spot outside for collecting rain where students do not usually play so that the rain gauges can be left undisturbed (see **Final Activities,** Step 4, on pg. 102). The spot should be clear of trees or building overhangs that would block precipitation. When you leave the rain gauges outside, it is a good idea to set them in a plastic crate or box to prevent their being blown over by the wind.

Procedure

1. Ask students if they remember the last time it rained. How much rain fell? Encourage them to recall where they noticed rainwater—perhaps in buckets or other containers that had been sitting outside.

Figure 10-2

Rain collected naturally

2. Introduce the idea of using a scale to measure rain. Explain that a rain gauge is a tool used for measuring rain, just as there are flags for estimating wind speed and thermometers for measuring temperature. Let students know that they will make their own rain gauges.

3. Distribute a copy of **Student Instructions for Making a Rain Gauge** to each pair of students. Then distribute a plastic cup and Unifix Cube™ scale to each student. Demonstrate how the Unifix Cube™ scale should be attached to the plastic cup.

4. Give pieces of clear packing tape to students when they are ready to put the scale on their cups. When students have finished making their rain gauges, distribute the pieces of masking tape on which they will write their names to identify their cups.

5. Take the class outside to the rain collection spot you have chosen. Tell the children that you are going to act as a rain cloud. Use the watering can or plastic carton to "rain" on each student's rain gauge. (Vary the amount of "rain" that you allow to fall on each gauge.)

6. As the students return to the classroom with their rain gauges, remind them to walk carefully so they do not spill the "rain." Students should place their rain gauges on a flat surface and look at them at eye level to read the scale measuring the amount of rainfall.

7. Ask students to tip their rain gauges to see what happens. Compare a tilted rain gauge with a level one. Then discuss why it is important for the rain gauges to be level when the rain is being measured.

8. Distribute crayons and two copies of **Record Sheet 10-A: Using a Rain Gauge** to each pair of students. Partners should help each other by checking and agreeing on the amount of water in their rain gauges. If necessary, help students transfer the information accurately onto the record sheets.

Final Activities

1. Show students the "Record of Rainfall" chart that you made to tally the rainfall data.

2. Have students raise their hand when the number of cubes that you call out (1 cube, 2 cubes, and so on) matches the amount of rain they collected. Use tally marks to record the results on the class chart.

3. Ask students if they think that a different amount of rain falls each time it rains. Point out that rain showers last different lengths of time and cover different amounts of space. Ask students how they think these factors might affect the amount of rain that falls.

4. Let students know that by using their rain gauges they can investigate whether the amount of rain varies. They will put their rain gauges in the rain collection spot and measure the rainfall each time it rains. These measurements can then be added to the Weather Calendar.

5. Place rain gauges in the collection spot today so they can catch unexpected, weekend, or evening rain.

Extensions
SCIENCE

1. Use the rain gauges as "snow gauges" on snowy days. Students can compare the amount of snow in the cup with the amount of water when the snow melts and discuss why there is less water than snow. (Snow is less dense than water; a cup of snow contains more air than a cup of water. When the snow melts, the air is released.)

LANG ARTS   SCIENCE

MATHEMATICS

2. Visit the library and look up information on plants that grow well with little rainfall.

3. Make a rainfall graph and keep track of how much or how often it rains. Figure 10-3 illustrates one way to make such a graph and shows some statements that summarize the information on the graph.

Figure 10-3

An example of a rainfall graph

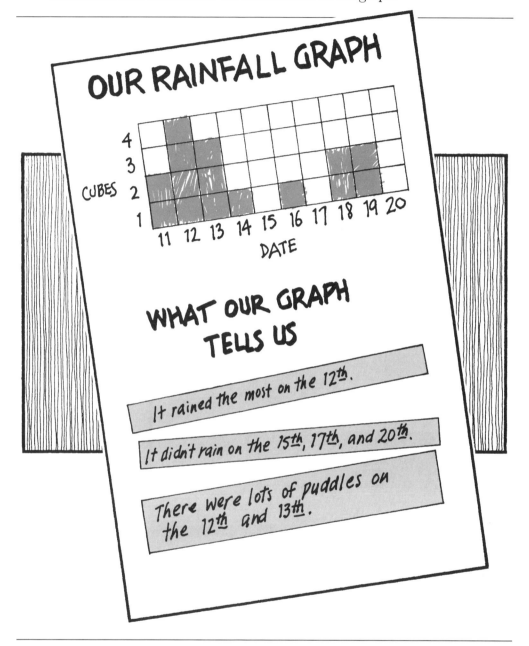

Assessment

Observational Guidelines

Your observations of your students working with their rain gauges will provide you with information about how well they can use this new tool and record data. Note the following:

- Do students use their rain gauges to measure the amount of rain?

- Do students read the rain gauge scales to the nearest cube?

- Do students transfer their reading of the amount of rainfall to their record sheets?

Student Instructions for Making a Rain Gauge

1. Lay the piece of tape on the table, with the sticky side up.

2. Have your partner place the scale on the tape with the cubes facing down.

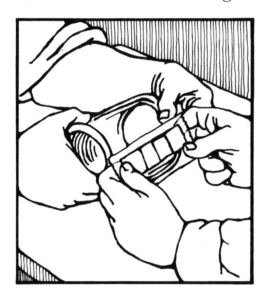

3. Have your partner hold the cup. Put the scale on the side of the cup. Be sure the bottom cube is at the very bottom of the cup.

4. Write your name on the masking tape. Put the tape on the back of the cup.

5. Now you have a rain gauge.

Record Sheet 10-A

Name: ---------------------------------

Date: ---------------------------------

Using a Rain Gauge

Color the picture to show how much rain you collected.

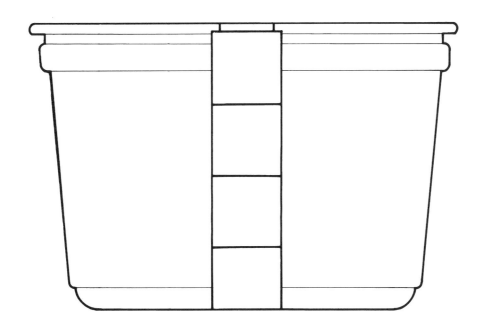

Rain Gauge Scales

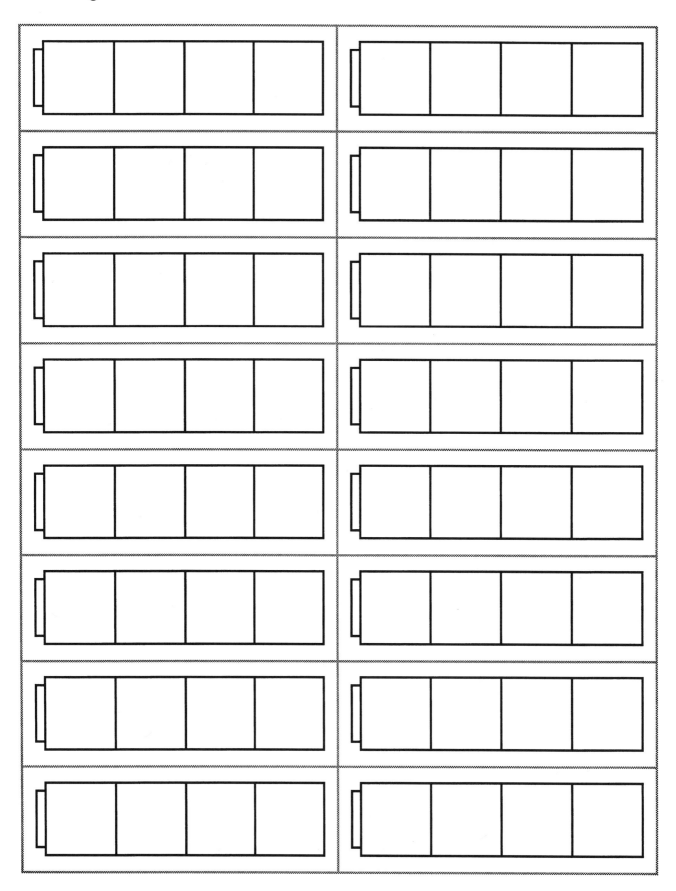

Exploring Puddles

Overview and Objectives

In the previous lesson, students learned how to use a rain gauge for collecting and measuring rainfall. They will now explore what happens to rain that has fallen and collected in puddles. Through their observations and discussions of the gradual disappearance of model puddles, students draw their own conclusions about what happens to water in puddles outside after it rains. Students further expand their understanding of weather by reading about the history of the umbrella and the invention of a special umbrella called the "Mud Puddle Spotter."

■ Students observe the process of evaporation.

■ Students record the changes in puddles that take place as the water evaporates.

■ Students read about and discuss the historical development of the umbrella.

Background

All water on earth is at one stage or another in the continuous cycle known as the **water cycle.** Water in the form of precipitation falls to earth. There it soaks into the ground or collects in large bodies such as oceans, rivers, and lakes. The sun heats up the water on earth and causes it to turn to water vapor, a gas, that rises. In other words, the water **evaporates.** As the water vapor rises, it is cooled, or **condensed,** turning back into liquid water. Precipitation then falls to earth again, and the cycle continues.

Young students should not be expected to understand the water cycle. However, they can easily observe that water disappears—evaporates—from a puddle. This initial exposure to the process of evaporation lays the foundation for studying the water cycle in later grades. A class discussion in this lesson will help students begin to develop their own theories about where the water goes when it disappears from puddles.

Materials

For each student
   1   copy of the blackline master **"My Puddle Book"**
   1   pair of scissors
       Crayons

For every four students
   1   aluminum pie plate, 20 cm (8 in) diameter
   1   small plastic cup, 118 ml (4 oz)

For the class

    2 pails of water

    Staplers

    Food coloring (optional)

    Paper towels or sponges

Preparation

1. Make one copy for each student of the blackline master **"My Puddle Book,"** on pgs. 117, 118, and 119.

2. Using the blackline master, make a sample of "My Puddle Book." Cut each page on the dotted line and staple all of the pages together on the left side.

3. Fill the two plastic pails with water. You might want to add food coloring to the water to make it more visible when it is poured into the pie plates. Put the pails, pie plates, and plastic cups on a table to create a distribution center.

4. Divide the class into groups of four students each.

5. Choose a sunny spot in the classroom where students can leave their pie plates and observe the puddles. Keep in mind that the duration of this activity will vary depending on classroom conditions, but it may take a few days to complete.

Procedure

1. Ask students to talk about where they see puddles when it rains. Ask them what happens to these puddles a day or two later. Where do the puddles go?

Figure 11-1

Observing a puddle

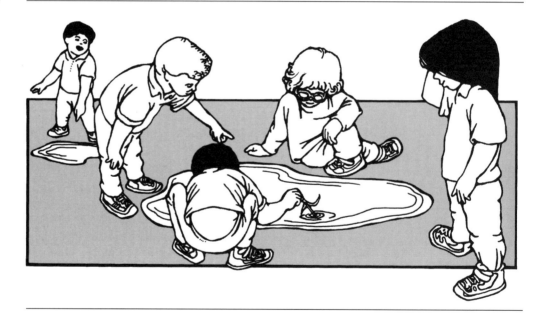

2. Show students the copy of "My Puddle Book" that you made earlier. Tell them that they are going to do an experiment with puddles and that they will use their own copy of "My Puddle Book" to record their data.

3. Distribute scissors, crayons, and a copy of the pages for "My Puddle Book" to each student. Have students cut the pages on the dotted lines and staple them together on the left side.

Safety Tip

You will need to supervise the students as they staple their books together.

4. Have students keep their copies of "My Puddle Book" and crayons at their desks and follow the steps below for the experiment.

■ Have one student from each group get one small cup of water from the distribution center.

■ Ask another student from each group to get one aluminum pie plate.

■ Have a third student pour the water into the pie plate.

■ Have all students record their first observation of the puddle in their own copy of "My Puddle Book" by coloring in the first picture so that it looks like the puddle in the pie plate.

■ Ask the fourth student in each group to take his or her group's pie plate with the puddle in it to the location in the classroom you selected. You may want to identify the puddles by putting a card listing the names of the children in each group next to their pie plate.

5. Ask students what they think will happen to the puddles. Then let them know that during the next few days they will observe their puddles and record their observations in "My Puddle Book."

Management Tip: Many factors, including room temperature, sunlight, and humidity, affect the rate of evaporation of the puddles. These factors will determine how frequently your class will need to make their observations. If the puddles disappear too quickly, have a class problem-solving discussion to try to identify the conditions that caused the rapid evaporation. Then do the experiment again under different conditions so that the students can observe and record the complete process.

6. Read **"Inventing Umbrellas,"** on pg. 113, to the class and discuss the following questions:

■ What else besides an umbrella do you use to keep dry on a rainy day? (Rubber boots, rain hat, raincoat.)

■ What do you think Katie's "Mud Puddle Spotter" looked like? Draw a picture.

Final Activities

As students observe their puddles and record their observations over the next few days, discuss these questions:

■ Where do you think the water went?

■ How long did it take each puddle to disappear completely?

■ Did all of the puddles disappear at the same time?

■ What would happen if some puddles had more water than others? Would the water disappear at different rates?

■ How are real puddles and the puddles in the pie plates alike? How are they different? Does the water go to the same place?

Extensions

MATHEMATICS

SCIENCE

MATHEMATICS

LANGUAGE ARTS

1. Make more model puddles that are of different sizes. Experiment to find out if they disappear at the same rate. If not, in what order do they disappear? Make a graph to show the results.

2. Take the class outside to observe puddles. Pick one puddle and designate it as the "class puddle." Ask students to predict what it will look like tomorrow. Then explain that you are going to outline the puddle with chalk so that they can compare the size of the puddle now with what it becomes later.

3. After a rainfall, ask the class to estimate how many puddles there will be on the playground. Define the area that you are considering. Then go outside and count the puddles. How did the estimate compare with the actual number? Use a daily graph to record observations; find out if all of the puddles disappear at the same time.

4. To help students explore puddles, read a book such as *The Rainy Day Puddle,* by Ei Nakabayashi. Ask students to write poems about puddles in their journals. You might invite them to help write a class story about puddles and have them illustrate each page to make a class book.

Reading Selection

Inventing Umbrellas

When Katie Harding was only five years old,
she became an inventor.
An inventor figures out how to make something new,
something that no one else has ever made before.
Katie figured out how to make a special kind of umbrella.
She called her invention a
"Mud Puddle Spotter."

What is a "Mud Puddle Spotter"?
Why did Katie invent it?

On rainy mornings when she
walked to kindergarten,
Katie carried a regular umbrella.
But sometimes she did not see
puddles as she walked along.
When she accidentally stepped in
the puddles, she got quite wet.
Her umbrella could not help
Katie with that problem.
Or could it? Katie had an idea.

"What about putting a light on my umbrella," she thought.
"A light would help me see the puddles on dark rainy mornings."

With her mother's help, Katie attached a flashlight
to her umbrella. Her idea worked!
Her invention helped her spot puddles as she walked to school.
Katie even won a prize for her "Mud Puddle Spotter"
in a contest for young inventors.

The very first umbrella was invented a long, long time ago.
It was probably made in China about three thousand years
before Katie made her "Mud Puddle Spotter."
We do not know the name of the person
who invented the first umbrella. But since then,
many other people have been interested in making umbrellas.
One of these people was Sir Jonas Hanway.

Sir Jonas lived in England about 250 years ago.
He was a businessman, and he often traveled to other countries.
When he went traveling, he saw people using umbrellas.
In England, most people did not have umbrellas.
They were expensive, and no factories made them.
He knew umbrellas were useful,
and he wanted people in his own country to be able to buy them.

Every day, Sir Jonas took a walk around London.
He always carried an umbrella.
The drivers of horse-drawn coaches were unhappy with Sir Jonas.
They wanted people to use coaches on rainy days, not umbrellas.
Some of them even drove through puddles and splashed him.
But that did not stop him from taking his daily walks,
umbrella in hand.

Sir Jonas also kept saying that all the people of London
should be able to have umbrellas to protect them from the rain.
And before he died, factories had been built
to make umbrellas for the people in England.
These umbrellas became very popular.
They were named for Sir Jonas. They were called "Hanways."

People seem to keep finding new ways to make umbrellas.
If you could invent a new kind of umbrella,
what would it look like?

My Puddle Book

BY _____

Day: _____

Day: - - - - - - -

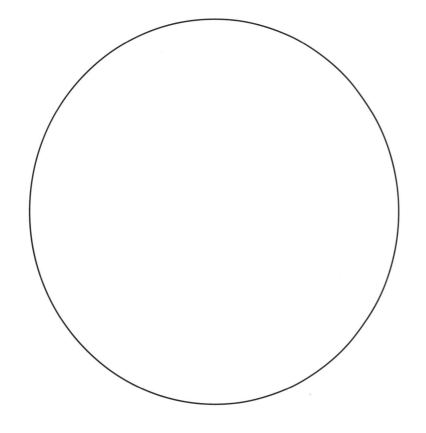

Day: - - - - - - -

Day: ------

Where did the water go? -------------------

Testing Rainy Day Fabrics

Overview and Objectives

The three lessons that focus on rain conclude with this one, in which students experiment with ways that different types of fabric respond to water. In discussing the results of their investigation, students use their observations to draw conclusions about which fabric would keep them driest on a rainy day. From a reading selection that describes the invention of waterproof cloth, students discover that rainy day fabrics have been the subject of experimentation for a long time.

- Students conduct an experiment with fabrics and water.

- Students record their results and draw conclusions.

- Students read about and discuss the history of the mackintosh raincoat.

Background

The fabrics selected for the activity in this lesson were chosen because they are typically worn by children—cotton, a cotton-polyester blend, wool, and nylon. In the experiment, each fabric is secured on top of a plastic cup. After pouring water over each fabric, students will observe two things: how much water has passed through the fabric into the cup and how wet the fabric feels. On the basis of these observations, the students can draw conclusions about which fabric would keep them driest on rainy days.

When a fabric becomes completely saturated, it can no longer absorb more water: any more water poured over it passes through it. Cotton and cotton-polyester absorb water quickly and become saturated almost immediately. This means that most of the water poured over them will pass through them, and because they are thoroughly saturated, they will feel very wet.

Wool absorbs water more slowly and takes longer to become saturated. Given its slow absorption rate and the small amount of water used in this experiment, little if any water will pass through the wool, although the wool will feel slightly damp. Nylon does not absorb any water. No water passes through the nylon; it feels very dry.

Note: The results of this experiment may vary depending on the thickness of each fabric, on the looseness or tightness of the weave, and on any chemical treatment that a piece of fabric might have received in manufacturing.

Materials

For each student

1 copy of **Record Sheet 12-A: Rainy Day Fabrics**
Crayons to match the colors of the four fabrics

For every four students

1 aluminum pie plate, 20 cm (8 in) diameter
1 small plastic cup, 118 ml (4 oz)
4 medium plastic cups, 296 ml (10 oz)
4 rubber bands
4 pieces of fabric (cotton, cotton-polyester, wool, and nylon) in different colors, 15 cm (6 in) square

For the class

2 plastic pails of water
Paper towels or sponges

Preparation

1. Make a copy of **Record Sheet 12-A: Rainy Day Fabrics,** on pg. 128, for each student.

2. Try the experiment before presenting it to the class so that you are familiar with the fabrics. It will be important to pour the water over the fabrics very slowly.

3. Divide the class into groups of four students each.

4. For easier distribution of the materials, put the materials for each group in a pie plate.

5. Place the pails of water where they will be accessible to more than one student at a time.

Figure 12-1

Caught in the rain

Procedure

1. Ask students the following questions: If everyone in the class went out in the rain today without an umbrella, whose shirt or jacket would keep them driest? Would everyone get just as wet as everyone else?

2. Encourage as many responses as possible. As the children respond, ask them to explain their answers; perhaps they have been caught in the rain.

3. Let students know that they will be doing an experiment to help them answer the questions and that the experiment will involve testing fabrics. Hold up each of the four squares of fabric and identify them as cotton, cotton-polyester, wool, and nylon. As you describe each type, point out any of the students' clothing made of that fabric.

4. Show students how to use a rubber band to secure a piece of fabric on a medium plastic cup, as illustrated in Figure 12-2. Explain that the experiment will involve working in groups of four, pouring water slowly over each piece of fabric attached to a cup, and observing certain results.

Figure 12-2

How to cover a cup with fabric

5. Point out that as they test each fabric, students should observe how much water goes through the fabric into the cup and how much spills over into the pie plate. They should also feel each fabric to see how wet it has become after the water is poured over it.

6. Distribute the materials for the experiment to each group. Have each member of the group select a piece of fabric and secure it on a cup with a rubber band.

7. Have the groups test one fabric at a time. One student from each group will first need to collect one small plastic cup of water from one of the pails. That student will slowly pour that one cup of water over the fabric as the others in the group observe and then feel the fabric to find out how wet it is. Students will need to empty the water from the pie plate into one of the pails or a sink before experimenting with the next fabric.

8. When the groups have completed the experiment, have them place their four cups in a row, so that the cup with the most water inside it is first and the cup with the least water is last.

9. Let each group share with the class what the order of their cups turned out to be. Also ask them to describe how wet or dry each of the four fabrics is.

10. Distribute crayons and a copy of **Record Sheet 12-A: Rainy Day Fabrics** to each student. On their record sheets, have students color the fabrics on the cups to match the real colors of their experiment fabrics. Then have them

color in the amount of water in each cup and write their responses to the questions on the record sheet.

11. Have students clean up by emptying the water in the cups into one of the pails or a sink.

Final Activities

1. Have students use the results of their experiment to discuss which fabric would keep them driest on a rainy day.

2. Read **"A Coat to Keep You Dry,"** on pg. 126, to the class and then discuss these questions:

   ■ What kinds of coats besides raincoats protect us from the weather? (For example, parkas and windbreakers.)

   ■ Many animals do not have feathers to protect them like birds do. What protects these animals from the weather? (For example, a bear's fur, snail's shell, elephant's thick skin.)

Extensions

SCIENCE

SCIENCE

MATHEMATICS

1. Have students set up an experiment to find out how long it takes each of the four fabrics used in this lesson to dry out completely. Ask them to discuss which fabric they would rather be wearing if they got caught in the rain.

2. Have students bring in other fabrics to test and then create a class chart to record which ones repel water best.

3. Brainstorm to come up with a list of rain gear. Make a graph entitled "Rainy Day Rain Gear," like the one shown in Figure 12-3. Have students put "X's" on the graph to show what kind of rain gear they use.

Figure 12-3

A rain gear graph

RAINY DAY RAIN GEAR

Number of Students

Rain Gear

Figure 12-4

An umbrella graph

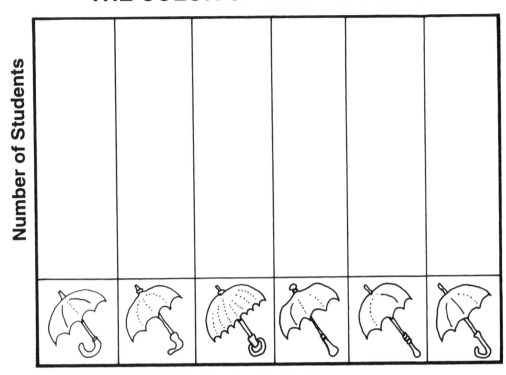

THE COLOR OF OUR UMBRELLAS

Number of Students

Umbrella Colors

MATHEMATICS

4. Make a graph entitled "The Color of Our Umbrellas," like the one illustrated in Figure 12-4. Let each student draw a picture of an umbrella, color it to match his or her own umbrella, and put it on the graph.

SOCIAL ST   LANG ARTS

5. To introduce students to another culture, read a book such as *Bringing the Rain to Kapiti Plain*, by Verna Aardema. Use a map to show the class where Africa is located. Talk about how the weather in different regions of Africa compares with your local weather.

Assessment

Observational Guidelines

Continue to listen for the spontaneous comments students might make about the weather and how it affects them. For example, notice whether they discuss the weather more frequently or whether they make specific comments about the clothes they are wearing in relation to the weather.

A Coat to Keep You Dry

Have you ever watched a bird sitting on a tree branch
in the warm summer rain?
Did you hear the bird singing cheerfully
as it fluffed up its feathers?

Would you be cheerful if you were out in the rain?
Would you be singing happily and skipping along?
Or would you be racing to get inside?

If you were wearing your raincoat,
you might be just as cheerful as a bird.
A bird's feathers keep it from getting "soaked to the skin."
Your raincoat keeps you from
getting soaked if you are
out in the rain.

Raincoats are made in a special
way to keep people dry.
They are made with
waterproof cloth.
Rain cannot go through
waterproof cloth.

The man who invented the first
kind of waterproof cloth
was named Charles Macintosh.
He lived in Scotland about two
hundred years ago.

This is how Mr. Macintosh made the cloth.
He knew that water would not go through rubber.
So, first he found a way to turn rubber into a liquid.
Then he painted the liquid rubber on a piece of cloth.
Another piece of cloth went on top.
When the rubber dried, the cloth and the rubber were
stuck together, like a peanut butter sandwich.
Water could not get through this cloth.
It was waterproof.

Mr. Macintosh soon began making raincoats with the new cloth.
People were very happy because his coats kept them dry.

The waterproof raincoat that Charles Macintosh invented
was named after him. It is called a "mackintosh."

Record Sheet 12-A

Name:

Date:

Rainy Day Fabrics

Color the fabric on each cup.

Color the cups to show how much water is in them.

| Cotton | Cotton-polyester | Nylon | Wool |

Which fabric would you wear in the rain?

Why?

Observing Clouds

Overview and Objectives

Since Lesson 3, students have been observing and recording information about cloud cover on the Weather Calendar as part of their daily observation of the weather. In Lessons 13 and 14, they take a closer look at clouds. Their observations increase their awareness of the many different ways clouds can look. This focus on the diversity of cloud shape and size prepares them for Lesson 14, when they classify three types of clouds.

■ Students observe and discuss clouds.

■ Students make three-dimensional pictures to record their observations of clouds.

Background

For the past several weeks, students have observed cloud cover as they collected weather data each day. They have recorded their observations of cloud cover on the Weather Calendar using the descriptions "sunny," "partly cloudy," "cloudy," and "foggy." In this lesson, besides observing cloud cover as a weather feature, students begin to focus on individual clouds and their appearance.

When you take your students outside to make their observations of clouds, they will have time to notice shapes and sizes and other cloud characteristics. These careful observations will help them become aware that clouds have many different shapes and sizes. You may want to consider taking students outside on several different days to expose them to a variety of cloud formations.

As students become more aware through their observations and through the activities in this lesson that not all clouds look alike, they are also preparing for Lesson 14. In that lesson they will explore a scientific way of looking at cloud differences. They will be introduced to the terms that meteorologists use to describe and classify three major types of clouds—stratus, cumulus, and cirrus.

Materials

For each student
- 1   sheet of light blue construction paper, 23 x 28 cm (9 x 11 in)
- 1   pencil
- 20 cotton balls
-     Glue or paste

For the class
- 1   sheet of newsprint
- 2   markers of different colors

Preparation

1. Plan to do this lesson on a day when there are clouds in the sky. Select a spot outside where students can either sit or lie down and quietly observe the clouds.

2. Divide the cotton balls so that each student has at least 20 of them.

Procedure

1. Begin this activity with a webbing exercise. Write the word "Clouds" on the sheet of newsprint. Encourage students to say what the word makes them think of, and record their comments on the web. Figure 13-1 illustrates some responses that you might expect from your class.

Figure 13-1

A class web on clouds

2. Take the class outside. Allow 5 to 10 minutes for students to observe the clouds in the sky. Encourage them to notice what the clouds are shaped like; how high they are; and what familiar things, such as animals, the cloud formations call to mind.

Safety Tip

Remind students not to look directly into the sun because it can be harmful to their eyes.

---

3. When you have returned to the classroom, invite students to share their new ideas about clouds. Add these to the web using a marker of a different color so that comparisons can be made between their ideas before and after they observe the sky.

Figure 13-2

Observing clouds

Final Activities

1. Distribute the blue construction paper, glue, cotton balls, and pencils to the class. Ask students to draw a picture of one cloud they observed. Then they can glue cotton balls on their pictures to make three-dimensional clouds.

2. Allow time for each student to tell the class about his or her picture.

Extensions

SCIENCE

LANGUAGE ARTS

LANG ARTS ART

1. Set up a demonstration center and "make" clouds. Boil water and then add ice cubes, which will produce steam (water vapor), or a "cloud." Hold a skillet lid above the boiling water and "rain" will condense on the lid.

2. After reading a book such as *It Looked Like Spilt Milk*, by Charles Shaw, compare the class pictures of clouds with those in the book.

3. As an introduction to an art project, read *Cloudy with a Chance of Meatballs*, by Judi Barrett. Have students draw clouds that look like food. Figure 13-3 illustrates two examples.

Figure 13-3

Clouds that look like food

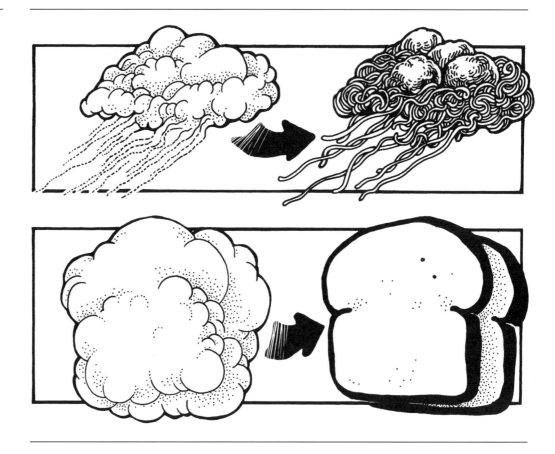

Classifying Clouds

Overview and Objectives

In the previous lesson, students described how clouds look to them. In this lesson they are introduced to the scientific terms for basic types of clouds: stratus, cumulus, and cirrus. So that students can see examples of all three types, they work with a set of cloud photographs in which each type is represented but not identified. This activity allows students to sort the cloud photographs using their own observations before they group these photographs in the three scientific categories.

■ Students create their own classification schemes for sorting cloud photographs.

■ Students sort the cloud photographs using the categories stratus, cumulus, and cirrus.

■ Students organize information about clouds on a classification chart.

Background

Clouds are collections of water droplets. The amount of water that they contain varies greatly, but, in general, puffy clouds contain more water than wispy ones. As mentioned in Lesson 13, the three main types of clouds are stratus, cumulus, and cirrus.

Stratus clouds, which form closest to the earth, are gray, characterless sheets of clouds. (Fog is a stratus cloud at ground level.) **Cumulus** clouds, which are higher than stratus clouds, resemble huge cotton balls. Cumulus clouds usually are associated with fair or good weather, but they can develop into thunderclouds. The highest clouds, **cirrus,** are made up of tiny ice crystals. They are wispy looking and are sometimes referred to as "mares' tails."

The differences among these types of clouds are so apparent that even young children will be successful at identifying them. Although meteorologists classify clouds in smaller, more precise groups, this simple classification system is sufficient for this unit.

Materials

For every three students
   1 set of nine cloud photographs

For the class
   1 copy of the blackline master **Cloud Classifications**

1 sheet of newsprint or poster board
Scissors
Tape or glue
Marker

Preparation

1. Decide which students will work together in groups of three.

2. You will want to become familiar with the nine cloud photographs before beginning the lesson. Notice that there is a number on the back of each to indicate cloud classification type: photos numbered 2, 6, and 9 are stratus clouds; 3, 4, and 7 are cumulus; and 1, 5, and 8 are cirrus.

3. Make one copy of the blackline master **Cloud Classifications,** on pg. 141. Cut out the three illustrations and mount them on the sheet of newsprint or poster board. Write the title "Cloud Classification Chart" at the top. Figure 14-1 shows the chart ready for class use.

Figure 14-1

A cloud chart

Procedure

1. Give each group of students a set of the nine cloud photographs. Challenge each group to sort the photographs into categories, putting clouds that look alike in each category.

2. Invite students to give each set of cloud photographs a name based on what the clouds look like to the group. Visit each group and ask students to explain their classification system.

3. Ask several groups to share their classification systems with the class. Have students explain why they grouped the pictures together and chose a certain name.

Final Activities

1. Show students the "Cloud Classification Chart." Point out the words "Stratus," "Cumulus," and "Cirrus." Let students know these are the words meteorologists use to describe clouds. Then describe what each kind of cloud looks like, using the information provided in the **Background** section, on pg. 137.

2. Ask students to look at the cloud photographs again and to organize the photographs according to the three categories shown on the "Cloud Classification Chart."

3. Ask students to brainstorm words they would use to describe each type of cloud. Write these words on the "Cloud Classification Chart" next to each cloud type.

4. Keep the "Cloud Classification Chart" on display in the classroom and have students add descriptive words as they continue to observe clouds.

5. Encourage students to write the formal cloud names on the Weather Calendar as part of their daily record keeping.

1. Have students write poems about clouds and draw cloud pictures on construction paper. Display these on a bulletin board.

2. Read a book that reinforces the idea of cloud classification, such as *The Cloud Book,* by Tomie DePaola.

3. Make a "Cloud Pop-up Book" with your class. For the directions, see Figure 14-2.

Assessment

Observational Guidelines

Although some of your students may enjoy using the scientific names for clouds introduced in this lesson, it is more important that they develop an awareness that there are different kinds of clouds. As students describe the clouds that they observe, ask yourself the following questions:

■ Do students describe differences in the clouds they see in the photographs?

■ Do students have a system for sorting the cloud photographs? Can they explain their systems?

■ Do students use descriptive words to characterize the three types of clouds?

■ Does students' awareness of clouds seem to increase after this lesson, as evidenced by more frequent and more descriptive comments about clouds?

Figure 14-2

*Directions for
making a cloud
pop-up book*

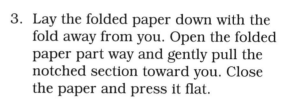

1. Make one page of the pop-up book
    for each student. Fold a piece of
    drawing paper in half. Punch two
    holes at the folded edge.

2. Cut two notches, about 2 inches
    apart, at the center of the fold.

3. Lay the folded paper down with the
    fold away from you. Open the folded
    paper part way and gently pull the
    notched section toward you. Close
    the paper and press it flat.

4. Open the paper. The cut-out section
    should look like a chair.

5. Have each student draw a picture of a
    cloud. Glue each cloud picture to the
    "chair" section of a page. This creates
    the pop-up. (The picture should extend
    less than halfway up the page so that it
    disappears when the book is closed.)

6. Have students color in the background
    and write a sentence beneath the cloud.

7. To assemble the book, glue the pages
    together. Make sure that the glue does
    not touch the pop-up part of the pages.

8. Finish the book by adding heavy
    sheets of paper or cardboard at
    the front and back for the cover.
    Write the title on the front cover.
    Punch holes at the edge of the
    cover and use rings or yarn to
    bind the book together.

Cloud Classifications

STRATUS	CUMULUS	CIRRUS

Comparing Forecasts to Today's Weather

Overview and Objectives

Throughout the unit, students have observed and described some basic features of weather. The activity in this lesson reinforces the close connection between students' new knowledge about weather and the world of meteorology. Comparing their own observations of today's weather with a meteorologist's forecast helps students recognize that the observable weather features they have become familiar with are the same features that meteorologists use in their daily forecasts.

- Students compare a weather forecast from the newspaper with the day's actual weather.

- Students discuss the fact that forecasts are predictions based on observed and recorded data.

- Students discuss ways that forecasts can help them make decisions about outdoor activities.

Background

A **weather forecast** is a prediction that a meteorologist prepares on the basis of previously observed and recorded data. Over the course of the *Weather* unit, your students, like meteorologists, have learned to observe several different weather features. Through the activities in today's lesson, they will discover that the local forecast reports on exactly the same weather features that they have been studying—cloud cover, precipitation, wind, and temperature. They see this clearly as they compare a forecast with their own observations.

It does not matter how closely the forecast matches students' observations of today's weather. As everybody knows, not all weather forecasts are accurate all the time. What is important is that students recognize that both they and the meteorologists observe the same features of weather.

Materials

For the class
- 1 sheet of newsprint or poster board
- 1 weather forecast from your local newspaper
- 1 marker
  Weather Calendar
  Temperature Graph

Preparation

1. From your local newspaper, save the weather forecast for the day you plan to teach this lesson. (For example, if you teach the lesson on Tuesday, bring in the forecast that appeared in Monday's paper.) Bring to class both the forecast and the section of the newspaper in which it appears.

2. On the sheet of newsprint, make a chart entitled "The Forecast and the Weather," like the one shown in Figure 15-1.

Figure 15-1

Chart for comparing forecast and weather

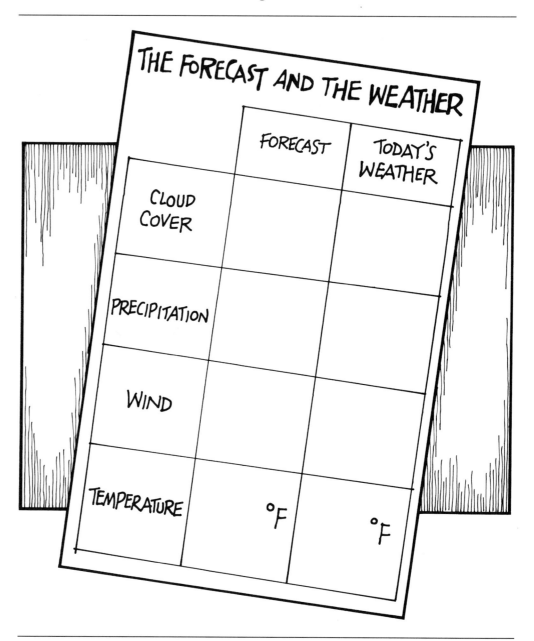

Procedure

1. Follow the usual daily procedure for gathering information about today's weather and recording it on the Weather Calendar and the Temperature Graph.

2. Invite students to discuss what they think the word "forecast" means. Remind them that Barbara McNaught, the meteorologist in the reading selection in Lesson 2, makes weather forecasts by using the information she gathers at the National Weather Service.

3. Show students the section of your daily newspaper that contains the weather forecast and read it to them. Explain that the class will compare the forecast from the newspaper with the information that the class has observed and recorded about today's weather.

4. Choose one or more students to write the data on the chart, "The Forecast and the Weather." Have them record the data from the newspaper and from the Weather Calendar and Temperature Graph.

5. Ask students to discuss any differences they see between the data they collected about today's weather and the forecast from the newspaper. For example, discuss some of these questions: Is the sun shining or is it overcast? Is there cloud cover today? Is there a light wind? Is it raining? What did the forecast predict?

Final Activities

1. Discuss the importance of forecasts in our daily lives, bringing today's forecast into the discussion. Ask the class to answer these questions:

   ■ How does a forecast help us decide what clothes to wear?

   ■ How can the weather forecast help us choose something fun to do outside with our family?

2. Invite students to share their ideas about the importance of weather forecasts for other people. You might introduce this topic by describing how forecasts help boaters and fishermen gauge whether it will be safe to be on the water on a particular day. Forecasts also predict weather at nearby vacation spots such as mountains or beaches and can help people make vacation plans.

Extensions

SCIENCE

1. To reinforce the classroom experience of comparing a forecast with the actual weather, send home with each student one copy of the blackline master **Recording the Forecast and the Weather,** on pg. 146. Have students fill out the column labeled "Forecast" with the help of someone at home. The next day, have students work together as a class to fill out the right-hand column, "Today's Weather."

SCIENCE

2. Compare radio, television, and newspaper forecasts with one another. Encourage students to speculate about why all the forecasts may not be the same.

LANGUAGE ARTS

3. Read a reference book such as *Weather Forecasting,* by Gail Gibbons, with the class. You may want to read only brief selections from the book at one time and then have a class discussion of that material.

Name: -

Date: -

Recording the Forecast and the Weather

	Forecast	**Today's Weather**
Cloud cover		
Precipitation		
Wind		
Temperature	°F	°F

Our Wind Scale
Weather Watchers
Look at the sky.
Is there any percipitation?
Is there any wind?
Our First Grade
of
WEATH
Questio
What Will the Weather Be?
Feel the W

Summarizing Our Weather Observations

Overview and Objectives

In this lesson, students' discussion of weather features they have observed over the course of the unit provides you with an opportunity to assess the growth in their knowledge of weather. Early in the unit, students were asked how one might remember what the weather was like two weeks before. Today they realize that they now have the information they need to answer this question. By examining the data from the Weather Calendar and Temperature Graph, they are able to summarize the weather over the past few weeks.

- Students review and discuss the data from the Weather Calendar and the Temperature Graph.

- Students tally collected weather data.

- Using their data, students summarize characteristics of the weather over a long period of time.

Background

One of the goals of the *Weather* unit is to help students collect, record, and interpret information. The activities in this lesson provide an opportunity for them to take part in interpreting the data that the class has been collecting over a long period of time. They will use the data on the Weather Calendar to form generalizations about what the weather has been like while they have been working on the unit.

The data might show, for example, that there were 30 sunny days, 4 partly cloudy days, and 6 cloudy days during that time. Using those numbers, students might formulate a statement like this: During our study of weather, most days were sunny. (It is important to remind the class that their conclusions reflect only the local weather for the period of time that their data were collected.)

In this lesson, students also examine the Temperature Graph. The graph may, over time, show a gradual change in temperature as the season changes. Sometimes, however, unexpected weather changes overshadow usual seasonal variations. If that happened while your class was studying the Weather unit, students can discuss and identify when variations occurred.

Materials

For each student
- 1   copy of **Record Sheet 16-A: Student Weather Tally**
- 1   copy of the blackline master **Super Meteorologist Award**
   Several completed Weather Calendar Post-it™ notes

For the class

1 sheet of newsprint
1 set of 11 weather stamps
1 marker
Weather Calendar
Temperature Graph
"Questions We Have about Weather" chart, from Lesson 2

Preparation

1. Make a copy of **Record Sheet 16-A: Student Weather Tally,** on pg. 155, for each student.

2. Make one copy of the blackline master **Super Meteorologist Award,** on pg. 156, for each student and fill it out. Decide how you want to present the awards to the students. (See Extension 1, on pg. 153, for ways to celebrate students' completion of the unit.)

3. Plan to distribute an equal number of Post-it™ notes from the Weather Calendar to each student. Figure out how many notes each will receive.

4. On the sheet of newsprint, make a chart with the title "Class Weather Tally," as shown in Figure 16-1. Use the 11 weather stamps to create the chart.

Figure 16-1

A weather tally chart

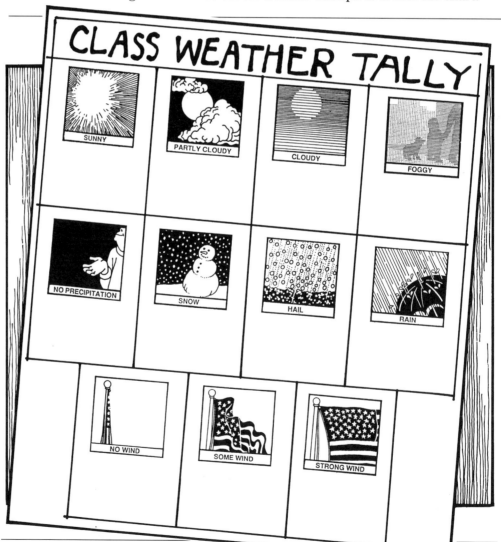

Procedure

1. Ask students what the weather was like two weeks ago. Invite one student to use the data recorded on the Weather Calendar to describe the weather at that time.

2. Show students the "Class Weather Tally" chart, and let them know that they will receive a record sheet that looks like this chart. They will use these record sheets to summarize the weather that was recorded on the Post-it™ notes from the Weather Calendar.

3. Using the "Class Weather Tally" chart, demonstrate to students how they will record the data from the Weather Calendar on their record sheets:

   ■ Choose a Post-it™ note from the Weather Calendar.

   ■ Read the weather data recorded on the note aloud to the class.

   ■ As you read, make a tally mark for cloud cover, precipitation, and wind in the appropriate space on the chart, as shown in Figure 16-2.

Figure 16-2

Tallying the weather data

4. Distribute a copy of **Record Sheet 16-A: Student Weather Tally** to each student. Also distribute the Post-it™ notes from the Weather Calendar to the students and have them record the data on their record sheets (see Figure 16-3).

5. Once students have completed their record sheets, help them compile all of the information on the "Class Weather Tally" chart. Call on each student to tell you how many tallies he or she marked in each section for cloud cover, precipitation, and wind.

6. Count the total number of tallies in each section of the class chart and record this number in the respective sections.

Figure 16-3

Filling out the record sheet

7. To help students summarize the data from the "Class Weather Tally" chart, discuss the following questions:

   ■ How many days were sunny?

   ■ Which type of cloud cover was most common?

   ■ Which type of cloud cover was least common?

   ■ What kind of precipitation was most common?

   ■ Were there any types of precipitation that did not occur at all?

   ■ How often was there no wind at all?

   ■ How often was there some wind or strong wind?

8. Now look at the Temperature Graph and discuss which temperatures were the most and least common. Highlight any temperatures that were unusually high or low.

Final Activities

1. To synthesize all of these data, have students help you write summary statements. For example, "The weather during the *Weather* unit was mostly cloudy with a lot of rainy days, and it was cold. There were only a few days of sunshine, and there was not much wind."

2. Invite students to look at the list of questions about weather they generated in Lesson 2 and added to during the unit. Which questions have been answered? Which questions have not been answered? Are there any they want to add today? Encourage students to continue learning about weather by investigating these questions.

3. Hand out the **Super Meteorologist Awards** to the students and celebrate their work as meteorologists! See Extension 1 for celebration ideas.

Extensions

LANG ARTS   ART

1. This final lesson provides an opportunity to celebrate your students' accomplishments as meteorologists. You might want to consider some of the following suggestions for a celebration:

   - Invite a meteorologist to present the **Super Meteorologist Awards** to the students.

   - Consider inviting others—either another class or the students' families—to participate in the celebration. Send them invitations in the shape of clouds, umbrellas, or raindrops.

   - Use a weather motif for the celebration—serve cloud-shaped cookies, for example, or decorate the room with snowflakes.

   - During the celebration, have students share what they have done and learned in the *Weather* unit.

LANGUAGE ARTS

2. Share a picture book about seasons, such as *Our House on the Hill,* by Phillippe Dupasquier. Children can make up their own stories to go with the pictures.

LANGUAGE ARTS

3. Have students create a "Crazy Flip Book" (see Figure 16-4).

Assessments

Throughout the unit you have had many opportunities to assess your students' growing awareness of the features of weather, their ability to use tools to measure weather, and their awareness of the effects of weather in their own lives. The Post-Unit Assessment and Final Assessments provide additional opportunities for your students to share what they have learned and for you to assess their growth.

Post-Unit Assessment

The Post-Unit Assessment (pgs. 157–158) is a matched follow-up to the pre-unit assessment in Lesson 1. Comparing students' pre- and post-unit responses to the same set of questions allows you to document their learning.

Final Assessments

Final assessments for this unit are on pgs. 159–163.

Figure 16-4

How to make a "Crazy Flip Book"

1. Compose a sentence about the weather that has three blanks for the students to fill in. Print the sentence on a long strip of paper. Leave enough space between the blanks so that later you can cut the strip into three sections. Give a copy to each student.

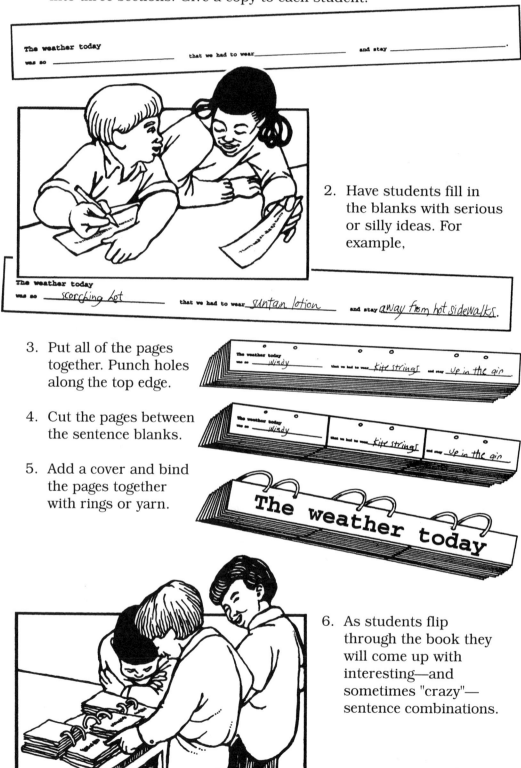

2. Have students fill in the blanks with serious or silly ideas. For example,

3. Put all of the pages together. Punch holes along the top edge.

4. Cut the pages between the sentence blanks.

5. Add a cover and bind the pages together with rings or yarn.

6. As students flip through the book they will come up with interesting—and sometimes "crazy"— sentence combinations.

Record Sheet 16-A

Name: --

Date: --

Student Weather Tally

SUNNY

PARTLY CLOUDY

CLOUDY

FOGGY

NO PRECIPITATION

SNOW

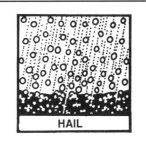

HAIL

RAIN

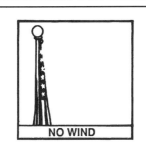

NO WIND

SOME WIND

STRONG WIND

WEATHER
Super Meteorologist Award

_____
Name

You're the Best

_____
Date

Post-Unit Assessment

Overview and Objectives

This is the second part of the matched pre- and post-unit assessment of students' knowledge of weather. In Lesson 1 during the first brainstorming session, the class developed two lists—"What is the weather like today?" and "How do you decide what to wear to school each day?" When students revisit these questions during the post-unit assessment, they have the opportunity to reflect on what they have learned about weather and how it affects their lives.

Post-unit brainstorming session

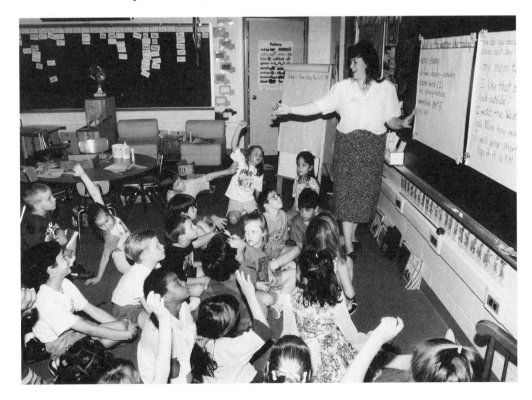

Materials

For the class

  2   sheets of newsprint

  1   marker

      Two class lists from Lesson 1

Preparation

1. At the top of one sheet of newsprint, write "Date," "Time," and "Location," with blanks for recording the date, time, and place the weather is observed. Also write the title on the chart—"What is the weather like today?"

2. On the second sheet of newsprint, write today's date and the question, "How do you decide what to wear to school each day?"

3. Have the class lists from Lesson 1 handy but do not display them until the end of the lesson.

Procedure

1. Ask students to share their observations of today's weather and record their responses on the chart "What is the weather like today?"

2. Now, ask students how they decide what to wear to school each day and record their responses on the second chart.

3. Display the chart "What is the weather like today?" from Lesson 1 and encourage students to compare their earlier responses with the ones they recorded today. Questions such as the following may facilitate your discussion:

   ■ How are your observations of weather today different from those in Lesson 1?

   ■ What are some weather features you observed today that you did not observe in Lesson 1?

4. Display the chart "How do you decide what to wear to school each day?" from Lesson 1 and encourage students to compare those responses with today's list. To facilitate this discussion, ask the following questions:

   ■ How did you decide what to wear to school each day in Lesson 1?

   ■ How did you decide what to wear today?

   ■ What is on today's list that was not on the list in Lesson 1? Has the way you decide what to wear changed?

5. As you compare the responses from Lesson 1 with those from today, look for detail in students' descriptions of weather and evidence that they consider the weather when deciding what to wear to school.

Final Assessments

Overview

Following are some suggested assessment activities. Although they are not essential, they can provide additional information for evaluating student learning. Consider using different kinds of assessments so that students with different learning styles will have additional opportunities to express their knowledge and skills.

- Assessment 1 asks students to pretend to be meteorologists reporting the weather and to suggest suitable clothing to go with the day's weather.

- Assessment 2 asks students to share with a visitor what they have learned about weather.

- Assessment 3 asks students to draw a picture and label it in answer to the question "What have you learned about weather?"

- Assessment 4 asks students to complete two record sheets similar to the ones completed in Lessons 5 and 6.

Assessment 1: Reporting the Weather

When students give a weather report, you have an opportunity to hear how they describe the weather, which weather features they mention, the detail in their descriptions, and the clothes they recommend for the type of weather they have reported.

Materials

For the class
- 1 set of 11 weather stamps
- 1 stamp pad
  Paper

Procedure

1. Give individuals or groups of students the task of making up the weather for a day, recording data on the weather features of their imaginary day, and then giving a weather report. Have them use the weather stamps in their presentations.

2. Invite students to make their weather presentations creative. They might use local maps, design a TV stage set, or create a weather observation station.

3. As part of their presentations, have students suggest clothing that might be suitable for the weather in their reports. They might also suggest appropriate outdoor activities—for example, "Today it is very windy. It would be good for flying kites."

4. Assess the weather features students include in their reports and the appropriateness of the clothing and activities they recommend.

Assessment 2: Tell a Visitor

For this assessment, students share with a visitor what they have learned about weather. This activity has proved to be an excellent way to assess what young students have learned about a specific topic. Teachers are often surprised at the extent of their students' knowledge.

Procedure

1. Invite a local meteorologist, your school principal, another teacher, parents, or another class of students to visit your class.

2. Encourage the visitor to begin the discussion by asking open-ended questions such as, "What have you learned about weather?" Then have that person ask more specific questions as students begin to share what they have learned.

3. Take notes on what students say during the visit and add them to your assessment file.

Assessment 3: Draw a Picture about the Weather

For this assessment activity, students draw a picture about the weather and label it in response to the question "What have you learned about weather?"

Materials

For each student
   Drawing paper
   Crayons or markers
   Pencil

Procedure

1. Distribute drawing materials to the students and ask them, "What have you learned about weather?" Have them respond to the question by drawing pictures or writing words. Students may want to draw more than one picture.

2. Look at each student's drawing for evidence of his or her knowledge of the weather topics discussed in the unit.

Assessment 4: Temperature Record Sheets

For this assessment, students complete record sheets similar to those in Lessons 5 and 6. Comparing the two sets allows you to document their growth in reading and recording temperatures shown on the record sheets. It also lets you see the growth in their awareness of clothing selection as it relates to the weather.

Materials

For each student
- 1 copy of **Record Sheet A-1: Reading the Temperature**
- 1 copy of **Record Sheet A-2: What Is the Temperature?**
- 1 red crayon

Preparation

1. Make one copy each of **Record Sheets A-1** and **A-2** (pgs. 162 and 163). Depending on your students' growth in reading thermometers and on the temperatures they have experienced during the unit, select two different temperatures and make a dark mark for those temperatures on the record sheets. (See the example of a marked thermometer on Record Sheet 5-A.) If your students can read temperatures in 2° increments, for example, you might want to mark one record sheet at 32°F and the other one at 96°F. (If you are using Celsius thermometers with this unit, mark them at appropriate temperatures.) If your students have not experienced noticeably different temperatures during the unit, just mark the thermometers at temperatures they actually have experienced.

2. For each student, make one copy of the record sheets you have marked.

3. Have available each student's copy of **Record Sheet 5-A: Reading the Temperature** and **Record Sheet 6-A: What Is the Temperature?**

Procedure

1. Distribute crayons and the copies of **Record Sheets A-1** and **A-2.**

2. Have students color the thermometers with the red crayon and then draw pictures on each of the record sheets.

3. Compare the finished record sheets with Record Sheets 5-A and 6-A. Look for progress in the students' ability to read and record temperatures. Reporting temperature to the nearest 10 is a reasonable goal for all students. Notice whether they label the temperature by writing "°F." Also assess whether their pictures show that they have developed more awareness of the correlation between temperature and certain clothing or activities. (Identifying clothing appropriate for a temperature shown on a thermometer is a more abstract process than knowing what to wear for certain kinds of weather.)

4. Consider having individual conferences with students so they can compare the record sheets along with you. Having students describe what they have written and drawn can be an effective way to obtain more detailed information as you assess their growth.

Record Sheet A-1

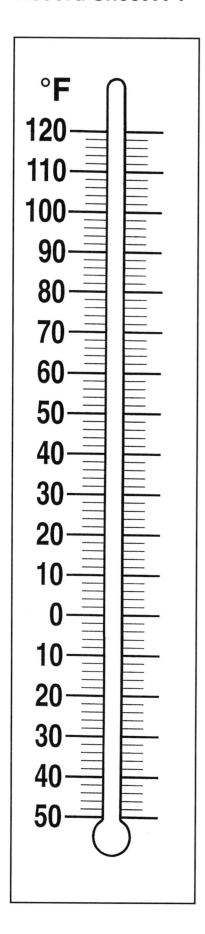

Name: --

Date: --

Reading the Temperature

What is the temperature?   ------------

Do you think this temperature is
hot or cold?

Record Sheet A-2

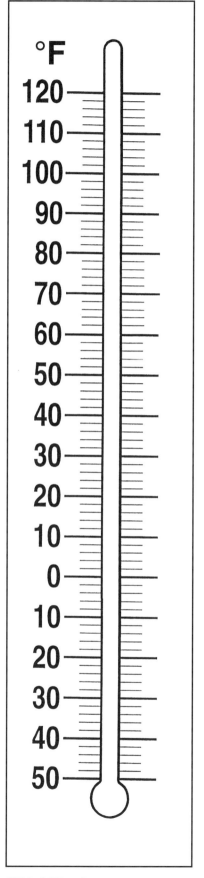

Name: ------------------------------

Date: ------------------------------

What Is the Temperature?

What is the temperature? - - - - - - - - - -

Do you think this temperature is
hot or cold?

Bibliography

The Bibliography is divided into the following categories:

- Resources for Teachers
- Resources for Students

While not a complete list of the many books written on weather, this bibliography is a sampling of books that complement this unit. These materials come well recommended. They have been favorably reviewed, and teachers have found them useful.

If a book goes out of print or if you seek additional titles, you may wish to consult the following resources:

Appraisal: Science Books for Young People (The Children's Science Book Review Committee, Boston).

> Published quarterly, this periodical reviews new science books available for young people. Each book is reviewed by a librarian and a scientist. The Children's Science Book Review Committee is sponsored by the Science Education Department of Boston University's School of Education and the New England Roundtable of Children's Librarians.

National Science Resources Center. *Science for Children: Resources for Teachers.* Washington, DC: National Academy Press, 1988.

> This volume provides a wealth of information about resources for hands-on science programs. It describes science curriculum materials, supplementary materials (science activity books, books on teaching science, reference books, and magazines), museum programs, and elementary science curriculum projects.

Science and Children (National Science Teachers Association, Washington, DC).

> Each March, this monthly periodical provides an annotated bibliography of outstanding children's science trade books primarily for pre-kindergarten through eighth-grade science teachers.

Science Books & Films (American Association for the Advancement of Science, Washington, DC).

> Published nine times a year, this periodical offers critical reviews of a wide range of new science materials, from books to audiovisual materials to electronic resources. The reviews are written primarily by scientists and science educators. *Science Books & Films* is useful for librarians, media specialists, curriculum supervisors, science teachers, and others responsible for recommending and purchasing scientific materials.

Scientific American (Scientific American, Inc., New York, NY).

> Each December, Philip and Phylis Morrison compile and review a selection of outstanding new science books for children.

Sosa, Maria, and Shirley Malcom, eds. *Science Books & Films: Best Books for Children, 1988-91.* Washington, DC: American Association for the Advancement of Science Press, 1992.

> This volume, part of a continuing series, is a compilation of the most highly rated science books that have been reviewed recently in the periodical *Science Books & Films.*

Resources for Teachers

Dishon, Dee, and Pat Wilson O'Leary. *A Guidebook for Cooperative Learning: Techniques for Creating More Effective Schools.* Holmes Beach, FL: Learning Publications, 1984.

> This practical guide was prepared to help teachers implement cooperative learning in the classroom.

Johnson, David W., Roger T. Johnson, and Edythe Johnson Holubec. *Circles of Learning: Cooperation in the Classroom.* Alexandria, VA: Association for Supervision and Curriculum Development, 1984.

> This book presents the case for cooperative learning in a concise, readable form. It reviews the research, outlines implementation strategies, and answers many questions.

Mogil, H. Michael, and Barbara G. Levine. *The Amateur Meteorologist: Explanations and Investigations.* New York: Franklin Watts, 1993.

> In this volume, written as a resource book for older students, teachers will find information about weather explained clearly and simply. Many of the suggested activities could be modified and used with young children.

Resources for Students

The following annotated bibliography is organized by subject.

Clouds

Barrett, Judi. *Cloudy with a Chance of Meatballs.* New York: Aladdin Books, 1978.

> This story about a place where rain falls in the form of food would be a delightful introduction to an art project in which students make "food clouds."

DePaola, Tomie. *The Cloud Book.* New York: Holiday House, 1975.

> This humorous approach to learning about different types of clouds contains inviting pictures and amusing comments that make it appealing to young children.

Shaw, Charles. *It Looked Like Spilt Milk.* New York: HarperCollins Children's Books, 1947.

> Each page in this book shows a cloud that resembles a different object. Students might benefit from looking at the book after they have observed clouds for themselves.

Rain

Aardema, Verna. *Bringing the Rain to Kapiti Plain.* New York: Dial Books, 1981.

> Rhythmic writing makes this story good for reading aloud. The book gives children an idea of life on an arid plain in Africa.

Bennett, David. *Rain.* New York: Bantam, 1988.

> This book presents a very simple explanation of the water cycle.

DePaola, Tomie. *The Legend of the Bluebonnet.* New York: G. P. Putnam's Sons, 1983.

> In this moving story for young readers, a Native American girl sacrifices her only possession, a doll, to get rain for her people. The rain comes and so do the beautiful bluebonnet flowers.

Ginsburg, Mirra. *Mushroom in the Rain.* New York: Macmillan, 1990.

> First one and then another animal seeks shelter under a mushroom in the rain. More and more animals come. How is it possible that they all fit?

Martin, Bill, and John Archambault. *Listen to the Rain.* New York: Holt and Company, 1988.

> The sounds of rain are described in poetic verse.

Nakabayashi, Ei. *The Rainy Day Puddle.* New York: Random House, 1989.

> In this simple introduction to the concept of evaporation, a frog enjoys his puddle as it gets larger in the rain and then watches as it gets smaller after the rain stops.

Serfozo, Mary. *Rain Talk.* New York: Macmillan, 1990.

> This book contains beautiful watercolor pictures and onomatopoeic text about a girl and her dog enjoying the rain.

Spier, Peter. *Rain.* New York: Delacorte Press, 1982.

> This picture book without words illustrates the activities of two children on a rainy and a very stormy day. It provides an excellent opportunity for having young children use descriptive language to tell the story shown in the illustrations.

Seasons

Dupasquier, Phillippe. *Our House on the Hill.* New York: Viking Press, 1988.

> This picture book illustrates the same outdoor scene each month throughout the year. Students can observe and discuss the changes that they see taking place in the landscape, people, and animals as the seasons change.

Hirschi, Ron. *Winter.* New York: Cobblehill Books, 1990.

> Beautiful photographs accompany brief text, creating a lasting impression of nature in winter.

Provensen, Alice, and Martin Provensen. *A Book of Seasons.* New York: Random House, 1982.

> Simple drawings show children enjoying seasonal outdoor activities. A Spanish version also contains the English text.

Rylant, Cynthia. *This Year's Garden.* New York: Macmillan, 1984.

> This book describes how one family cares for its garden throughout the year-long cycle, from planning in the winter to planting in the spring. The book includes pictures for each season.

Selsam, Millicent. *Where Do They Go? Insects in Winter.* New York: Scholastic, 1981.

> Informative drawings and text answer the question of where insects go in winter.

Van Allsburg, Chris. *The Stranger.* New York: Houghton Mifflin, 1986.

> Beautiful pictures illustrate the coming of autumn.

Snow

Betterworth, Nick. *One Snowy Night.* New York: Little, Brown, 1990.

> Pictures that young children find particularly appealing enhance this story about protecting woodland animals from the cold.

Branley, Franklyn. *Snow Is Falling.* New York: Harper and Row, 1986.

> The book describes the hazards and the usefulness of snow.

Hader, Berta, and Elmer Hader. *The Big Snow.* New York: Macmillan, 1976.

> This book explains how animals cope with the winter cold and describes how animals that remain active find food.

Harshman, Marc. *Snow Company.* New York: Cobblehill Books, 1990.

> This is a story, with excellent illustrations, of people helping one another during a storm.

Keats, Ezra Jack. *The Snowy Day.* New York: Viking Press, 1962.

> This Caldecott Medal winner tells the story of Peter's day in the snow. Its illustrations are closely integrated with the text.

Storms

Branley, Franklyn. *Tornado Alert.* New York: HarperCollins, 1990.

> This informative book about the origin and characteristics of tornadoes includes helpful safety tips.

Carrick, Carol. *Lost in the Storm.* New York: Houghton Mifflin, 1979.

> As two friends take refuge during an unexpected storm, the weather conditions before, during, and after the storm are described.

Mayer, Mercer, and Gina Mayer. *Just a Thunderstorm.* Racine, WI: Western Publishing, 1993.

> This little book illustrates the fear children often feel in a thunderstorm. As the character discovers, however, thunderstorms do create great mud puddles.

Parker, Mary Jessie. *City Storm.* New York: Scholastic, 1990.

> Lovely watercolor pictures show how a scene changes before, during, and after a storm.

Zolotow, Charlotte. *The Storm Book.* New York: HarperCollins Children's Books, 1952.

> This Caldecott Medal winner, to be read to young children, helps them imagine a summer storm as it affects the country, the city, and the beach. The author's beautiful prose can introduce students to the power of imagery in writing.

Wind

Ets, Marie Hall. *Gilberto and the Wind.* New York: Penguin, 1986.

> Gilberto discovers a multitude of activities that are fun to do in the wind. He sails a toy boat, flies a kite, blows bubbles, and more. This book is also available in Spanish.

Hutchins, Pat. *The Wind Blew.* New York: Penguin, 1986.

> The book tells the tale of a wind that temporarily carries off hats, umbrellas, scarves, and anything else in its path.

Poetry

Frank, Josette. *Snow Toward Evening.* New York: Dial Books, 1990.

> In this anthology, 13 nature poems by famous poets are accompanied by excellent watercolor illustrations.

Pretulusky, Jack. *Random House Book of Poetry.* New York: Random House, 1983.

> Poems for young children are presented in the section on "The Four Seasons" in this anthology.

Schenk de Regniers, Beatrice. *Sing a Song of Popcorn.* New York: Scholastic, 1988.

> This anthology includes a section entitled "Mostly Weather," which contains poems for young children. The illustrations are by Caldecott Medal-winning artists.

Miscellaneous

Gibbons, Gail. *Weather Forecasting.* New York: Macmillan, 1987.

> In this behind-the-scenes look at a forecasting station, each descriptive picture has a caption, and technical words are boldfaced.

———. *Weather Words.* New York: Holiday House, 1990.

> Illustrations accompany each weather word and definition in this reference book for young children.

Maestro, Betsy, and Giulio Maestro. *Temperature and You.* New York: Lodestar Books, 1990.

> The simple text and drawings explain the concept of temperature. Specific temperatures (in both Fahrenheit and Celsius) are matched with illustrations of appropriate outdoor activities, such as swimming and sledding.

Rogers, Paul. *What Will the Weather Be Like Today?* New York: Greenwillow Books, 1989.

> This book with simple, rhyming text illustrates different types of weather in different places, from the country to the steamy, hot rain forest. The pictures also show activities such as picnicking or skiing for different types of weather.

The Development of the Fahrenheit and Celsius Scales

The purpose of this appendix is to provide brief supplementary information for teachers on the development of the Fahrenheit and Celsius scales. As mentioned in Lesson 5, these scales are the two most widely used for measuring temperature—the Fahrenheit scale being used only in the United States, the Celsius scale throughout the rest of the world.

The Fahrenheit Scale

By the time Gabriel Daniel Fahrenheit (1686–1736) invented his successful thermometer scale, scientists in Europe had been experimenting with temperature scales for about 100 years. But no one had yet developed a standard scale that would allow people in different places to compare temperatures, so the usefulness of the thermometer as a scientific instrument was limited. Since Fahrenheit himself was a maker of meteorological and other scientific instruments, the problem interested him. As we know from using the temperature scale that bears his name, he succeeded in solving it.

Before inventing his scale, however, Fahrenheit made another important contribution to the development of the thermometer: he made the instrument accurate by figuring out how to use mercury in its tube instead of alcohol or the alcohol-water mixtures that were used then. The problem with these substances was that alcohol boiled at temperatures too low to allow high temperatures to be measured, and alcohol-water mixtures expanded unevenly with changing temperature. Mercury expanded evenly, contributing to greater accuracy. Makers of thermometers before Fahrenheit tried using mercury, but they were unsuccessful. The problem with mercury was that it clung to the walls of the glass thermometer tube, preventing accurate measurement. In 1714, Fahrenheit found a way to purify mercury so this would not happen.

Over the next 10 years, Fahrenheit worked out his temperature scale. To calibrate his thermometer and then define a scale, he needed two fixed reference points—that is, a low and a high point between which to divide the scale into degrees. At first, he used the freezing point of a water-salt mixture, which he designated as 0°, and normal human body temperature, which he designated as 96°. (At that time, the freezing point of a water-salt mixture was widely considered to be the coldest possible temperature.)

Fahrenheit divided the interval between the two reference points into 96 equal units, or degrees. In 1724, he made a change; he set the freezing point of water, 32°, as the lower reference. On this scale, Fahrenheit determined that water boiled at 212°, but he did not use that as one of his fixed references. However, by about 1740—a few years after Fahrenheit's death—the boiling point of water was widely used as the upper reference. On the modern Fahrenheit scale, with the fixed points set at 32° and 212°, normal body temperature is 98.6°.

When Fahrenheit reported on his scale in 1724, it was immediately adopted in Great Britain and the Netherlands, becoming the first successful standard temperature scale. It is still used for meteorological and other purposes in the United States.

Figure A-1

The freezing point and the boiling point of water on the Fahrenheit and Celsius scales

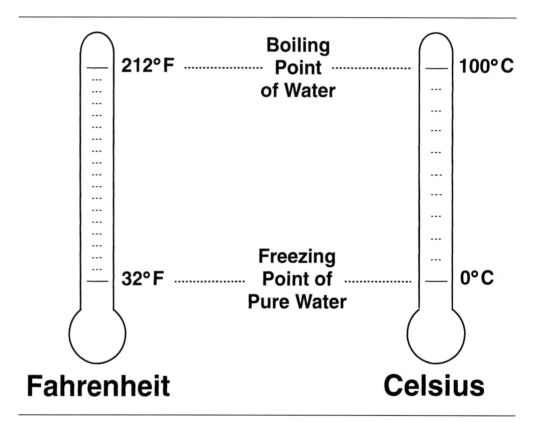

The Celsius Scale

Unlike Fahrenheit, Anders Celsius (1701–1744) did not develop a new type of thermometer, but he did invent another famous temperature scale. Celsius, a Swedish astronomer, invented his scale in 1742. It has become the most widely used scale in the world, and it is used by scientists in all countries.

For many years this scale was known as the centigrade (or 100-step) scale. The name reflects its convenient division into exactly 100 degrees between the freezing and boiling points of water. Temperatures below the freezing point of water are shown as negative numbers. This division is appealing because it is less complicated than the 180 degrees between these two points on the Fahrenheit scale.

When Celsius originally devised his scale, he put the boiling point at 0° and the freezing point at 100°. The scale was inverted shortly thereafter—0° became the freezing point and 100° became the boiling point.

Celsius's scale continued to be called centigrade for almost 200 years after its invention. Then, in 1948, the Ninth General Conference of Weights and Measures ruled that it would be officially called the Celsius scale. Nonetheless, both names are commonly used today.

Celsius Record Sheets and Blackline Masters

If you have elected to use the Celsius scale in teaching the *Weather* unit, you will want to use the record sheets and blackline masters contained in this appendix. They are

Record Sheet 5-A

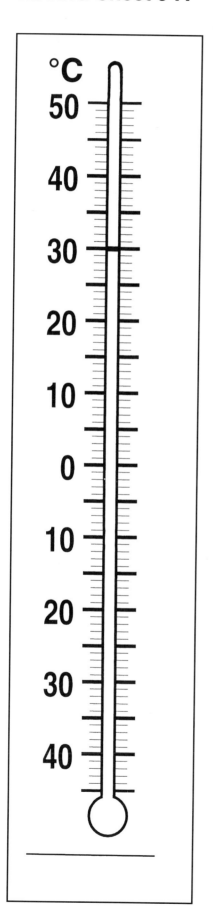

Name: ------------------------------

Date: ------------------------------

Reading the Temperature

What is the temperature? -------- °C

Do you think this temperature is
hot or cold?

Large Model Celsius Thermometer (top section)
Note: Figure 5-1 in Lesson 5 gives directions for constructing a large model thermometer.

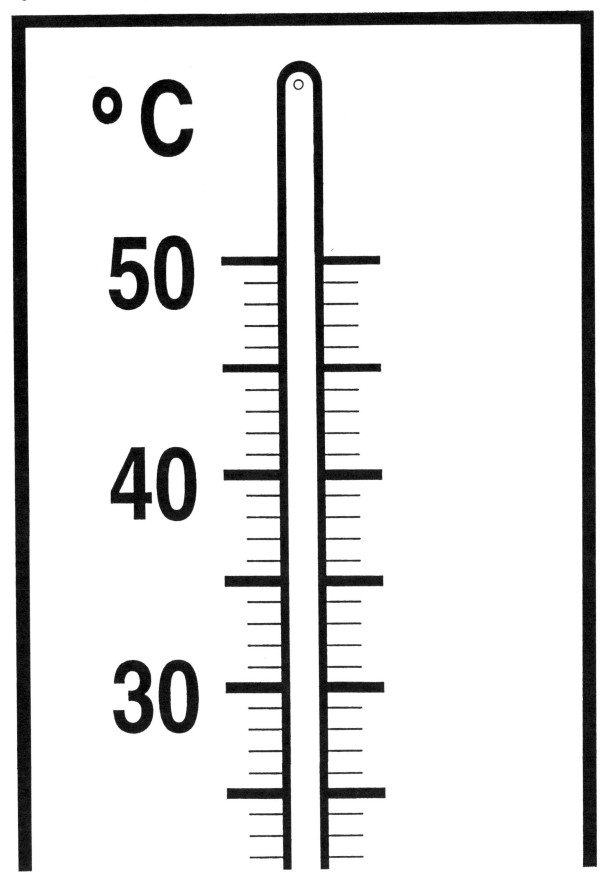

Large Model Celsius Thermometer (middle section)

Large Model Celsius Thermometer (bottom section)

Record Sheet 6-A

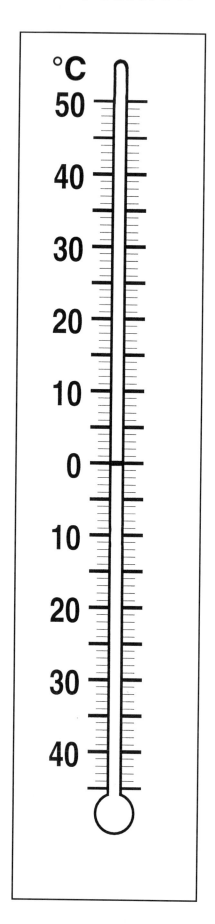

Name: _____

Date: _____

What Is the Temperature?

What is the temperature? _ _ _ _ _ _ _ °C

Do you think this temperature is
hot or cold?

_____

_ _ _ _ _ _ _ _ _ _ _ _ _ _ _ _ _ _ _ _

Record Sheet 7-A

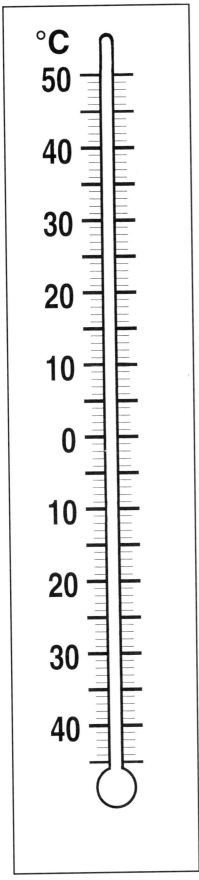

Name: -

Date: -

Recording the Temperature Inside

The temperature inside is - - - - - - - - - - - .

Color this temperature on the thermometer.

Record Sheet 7-B

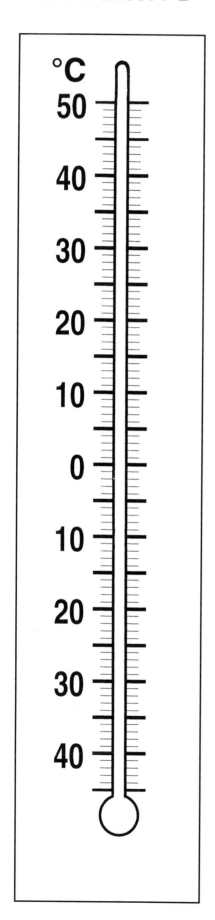

Name: _____

Date: _____

Recording the Temperature Outside

The temperature outside is _____.

Color this temperature on the thermometer.

Record Sheet 8-A

Graphing
Water Temperature

°C

Name: -

Date: -

50

40

30

20

10

0

10

20

30

40

Cold Water   **Hot Water**   **Mixed Water**

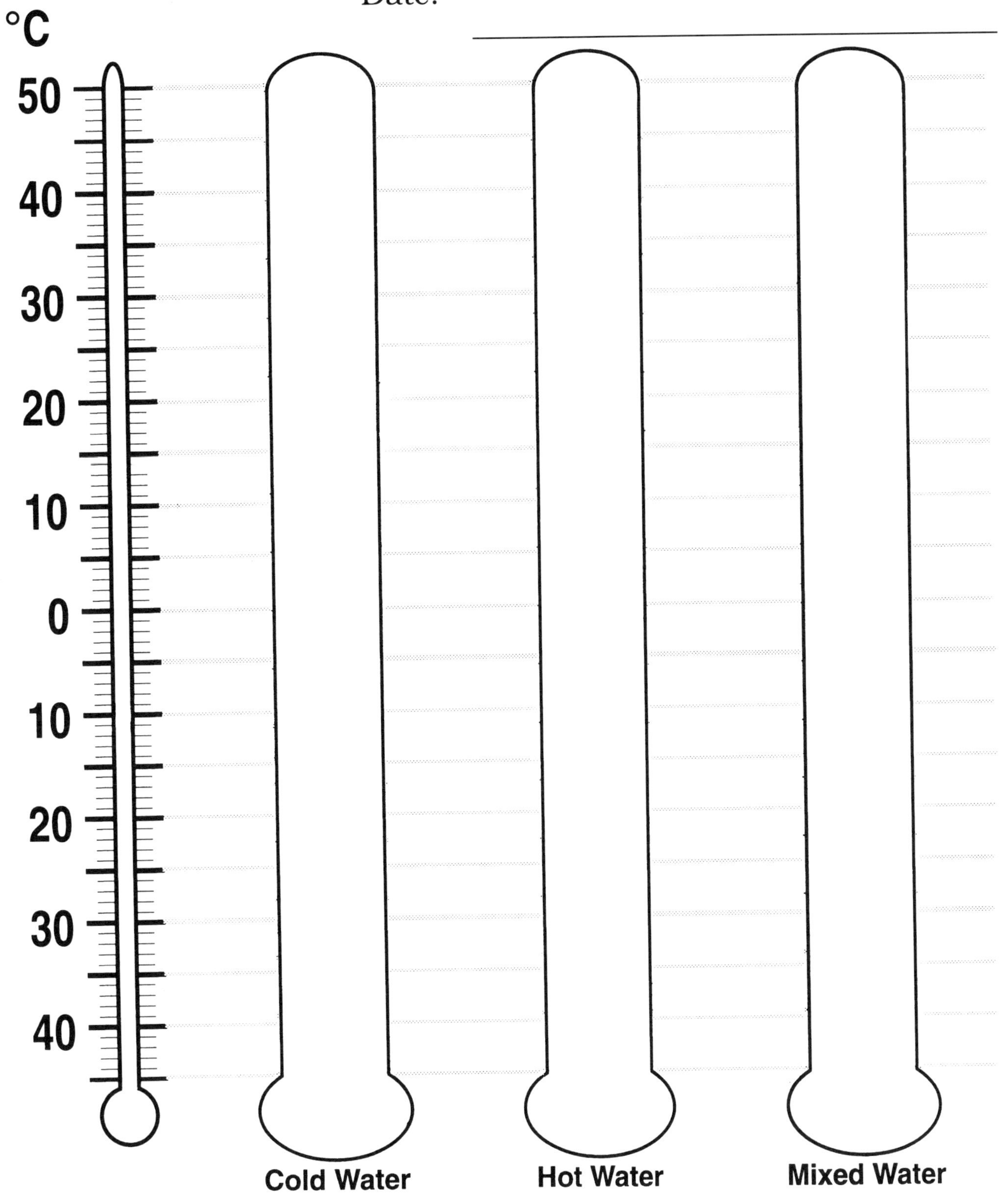

Cold Water Place Mat

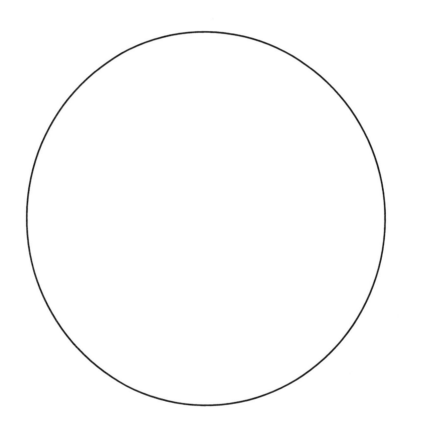

°C

_____

Hot Water Place Mat

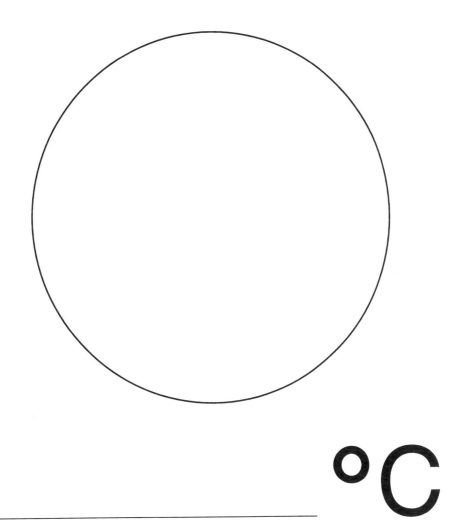

°C

_____

Mixed Water Place Mat

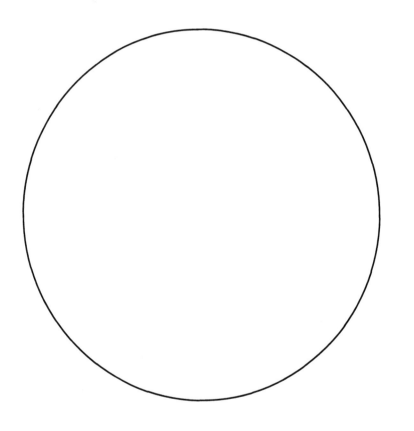

°C

_____

Name: -

Date: -

Recording the Forecast and the Weather

	Forecast	**Today's Weather**
Cloud cover		
Precipitation		
Wind		
Temperature	°C	°C

Record Sheet A-1

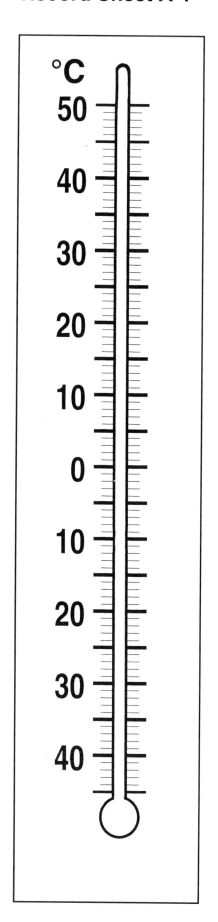

Name: _____

Date: _____

Reading the Temperature

What is the temperature?

Do you think this temperature is
hot or cold?

_____

_____

Record Sheet A-2

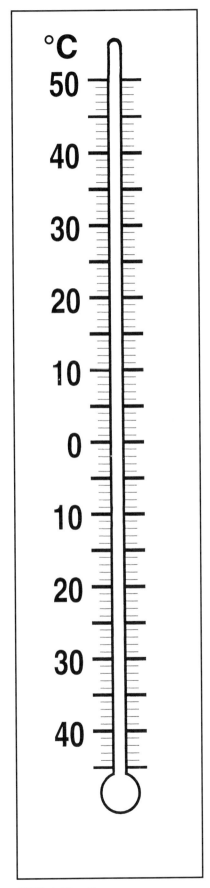

Name: --

Date: --

What Is the Temperature?

What is the temperature? -----------

Do you think this temperature is
hot or cold?

National Science Resources Center Advisory Board

Chairman

Robert M. Fitch, Senior Vice President (retired), Research and Development, S. C. Johnson Wax, Racine, WI

Members

Russell Aiuto, Senior Project Officer, Council of Independent Colleges, Washington, DC

Marjory Baruch, Educational Consultant, Fayetteville, NY

Ann Bay, Director, Office of Elementary and Secondary Education, Smithsonian Institution, Washington, DC

DeAnna Banks Beane, Project Director, YouthALIVE, Association of Science-Technology Centers, Washington, DC

F. Peter Boer, Executive Vice President and Chief Technical Officer, W. R. Grace and Company, Boca Raton, FL

Douglas K. Carnahan, Vice President and General Manager, Measurement Systems Organization, Hewlett-Packard Company, Boise, ID

Fred P. Corson, Vice President and Director, Research and Development, The Dow Chemical Company, Midland, MI

Goéry Delacôte, Executive Director, The Exploratorium, San Francisco, CA

JoAnn E. DeMaria, Elementary School Teacher, Hutchison Elementary School, Herndon, VA

Hubert M. Dyasi, Director, The Workshop Center, City College School of Education (The City University of New York), New York, NY

Bernard S. Finn, Curator, Division of Electricity and Modern Physics, National Museum of American History, Smithsonian Institution, Washington, DC

Gerald D. Fischbach, Department of Neurobiology, Harvard Medical School, Boston, MA

Samuel H. Fuller, Vice President of Corporate Research, Digital Equipment Corporation, Littleton, MA

Ana M. Guzmán, Program Director, Alliances for Minority Participation, Texas A & M University, College Station, TX

Robert M. Hazen, Staff Scientist, Carnegie Institution of Washington, Washington, DC

Norbert S. Hill, Jr., Executive Director, American Indian Science and Engineering Society, Boulder, CO

Manert Kennedy, Executive Director, Colorado Alliance for Science, University of Colorado, Boulder, CO

John W. Layman, Professor of Education and Physics, and Director, Science Teaching Center, University of Maryland, College Park, MD

Sarah A. Lindsey, Science Coordinator, Midland Public Schools, Midland, MI

Thomas E. Lovejoy, Counselor for Biodiversity and Environmental Affairs, Smithsonian Institution, Washington, DC

Lynn Margulis, Professor of Biology, Department of Botany, University of Massachusetts, Amherst, MA

Shirley M. McBay, President, Quality Education for Minorities Network, Washington, DC

John A. Moore, Professor Emeritus, Department of Biology, University of California, Riverside, CA

Philip Needleman, Corporate Vice President, Research and Development, and Chief Scientist, Monsanto Company, St. Louis, MO

Carlo Parravano, Director, Merck Institute for Science Education, Rahway, NJ

Ruth O. Selig, Executive Assistant to the Acting Provost, Smithsonian Institution, Washington, DC

Maxine F. Singer, President, Carnegie Institution of Washington, Washington, DC

Paul H. Williams, Director, Center for Biology Education, and Professor, Department of Plant Pathology, University of Wisconsin, Madison, WI

Karen L. Worth, Faculty, Wheelock College, and Senior Associate, Urban Elementary Science Project, Education Development Center, Newton, MA

Ex Officio Members

E. William Colglazier, Executive Officer, National Academy of Sciences, Washington, DC

James C. Early, Assistant Provost for Educational and Cultural Programs, Smithsonian Institution, Washington, DC